BLACK HILLS BADLANDS

The Web of the West

Text by Mike Link
Photographs by
Craig Blacklock

with Les Blacklock

Voyageur Press

ISBN 0-89658-017-2

Printed in Hong Kong

93 94 95 96 97 8 7 6 5 4

Published by
VOYAGEUR PRESS
P.O. Box 338, 123 North Second Street
Stillwater, Minnesota 55082 USA

Please write or call, or stop by, for our free catalog of natural history, photography, and cooking-related publications. Our toll-free number to place an order or to request a free catalog is 800-888-9653 (or call 612-430-2210 from Minnesota, Alaska, Hawaii, and Canada).

Educators, fundraisers, premium and gift buyers, publicists, and marketing managers: Looking for creative products and new sales ideas? Voyageur Press books are available at special discounts when purchased in quantities, and special editions can be created to your specifications. For details contact our marketing department.

Contents

PART I — INDIAN IMAGES   5
1   Web of the Hills   7
2   The Badlands   10
3   The Grassland Indians   12
4   Fort Meade   14
5   The Sky Pillars   19
6   Fort Robinson   22

PART II — THE LURE OF THE MOUNTAINS   41
7   The Black Mountains   42
8   The Canyons   44
9   Gold   45
10   Windows without Glass   46

PART III — THE WILD WEST   65
11   The Black Hiller   67
12   Wild Horse Harry Hardin and Poker Alice   68
13   Bob Brislawn and The Sundance Kid   70
14   Deadwood   72
15   Wild Bill Hickok, Calamity Jane, and Preacher
      Smith   73
16   The Heroes of Deadwood   76
17   Deadwood to Cheyenne   79

PART IV — ALWAYS THE HILLS   89
18   Wanderings   91
19   The Four Faces of Paradox   92
20   The Naturalists   94
21   Song of the Land   113
22   A Closing Reflection   116
BIBLIOGRAPHY   117

PART I —

INDIAN IMAGES

CHAPTER 1 # WEB OF THE HILLS

While I drove across freshly washed grasslands, pronghorns dashed like zephyrs over the grassy knolls. The whiteness of their rumps seemed to shine in the misty morning greyness as though giving off their own light independent of the sun.

The storm that had dampened the land was a cyclonic system of great cloud arms, stretched like the tentacles of a great galaxy, reaching to each horizon. I drove in and out of sun and shade, past sage sparrows and chestnut collared longspurs perched on wooden fence posts. A mule deer doe and two fawns scrambled away from my presence. The body of the swirling system moved like a great flying machine toward the heart of The Hills, but the grey tentacles reached to the surrounding prairies. This web encompassed the region.

Like the storm, The Hills reach out in each direction, a giant web of life. Streams pick up water in the highlands and roll to the lowlands. Indians living in Wyoming, Dakota, and Nebraska all find spiritual and physical stores in the mountains.

The web of The Hills is often woven with strong personalities, and these characters reflect the variations of the land. Vincent McGillycuddy was like that. He was a strong-willed adventurer whose name is associated with Fort Laramie, Slim Buttes, Deadwood, Rapid City, Fort Robinson, and Pine Ridge. His personal story is as much a biography of the land and times as it is a story of the individual.

McGillycuddy was a medical doctor at the Marine Hospital in Detroit in 1866 when he discovered that he had a weak heart. In this period of history doctors had replaced the clergy as a professional branch of natural history. The doctor had to know plants and anatomy, and this made him a good observer of natural phenomenon, so government expeditions liked to have medical personnel along for both notation and immediate health insurance. The doctor was likely to prescribe nature, exercise, and fresh air as a curative for many ills, including his own. This combination changed Dr. McGillycuddy from Detroit surgeon to adventurer.

He signed on as assistant engineer and recorder for the geodetic survey of Northern and Northwestern Lakes of Michigan, got caught in a nor'easter three miles offshore in Lake Michigan, surveyed Chicago after the fire of 1871, and joined Major Twining to survey the United States-British boundary. His health had improved, and his job was topographer and surgeon.

In the west he became a surveyor for a four-man research and recognizance party from Fort Laramie that was to confirm or deny Custer's claim of gold in The Black Hills. Henry Newton and Walter Jenny of the Columbia School of Mines, and Horace Tuttle of the Naval Observatory in Washington, D.C., were the other three men in the team. This was to be McGillycuddy's introduction to The Hills.

In the party's military escort was a woman who was disguised as an army private. After being discovered, she was ordered out of uniform and told to leave the party. This meant that she shifted to tag-a-long and ended up caring for the sick and mending clothes during the expedition. The men called her Calamity Jane.

For McGillycuddy the expedition was only the beginning of a long association with The Hills legends. He joined General Crook as a field doctor, fought at the Battle of the Rosebud, and later joined Terry's epic march of deprivation to Deadwood. New saddle sores were marked with chalk each night, and holes were cut in the saddle pads. When rations ran out after only five days, the men tried eating prairie dogs, but became very ill. They shot and ate the horses and made mush from prickly pear cactus.

On this particular march McGillycuddy was part of the Battle of Slim Buttes and witnessed the death of Charlie White, a scout called Buffalo Chips because of his friendship with Buffalo Bill. He also operated on Chief American Horse, who died soon after surgery.

The troops eventually arrived to a heroes' welcome in Deadwood, and among the celebrities who met them were Calamity Jane and Sheriff Seth Bullock.

McGillycuddy had the task of taking insane soldiers to the National Asylum in Washington, D.C. He visited his wife in Detroit before returning to The Hills where his next assignment was Assistant Post Surgeon at Fort Robinson, the Fort where Crazy Horse would die.

The Indian Agencies were a hotbed of organized crime, with the "Indian Ring" peddling influence money in Washington. Agents on the reservations and men in the Washington Bureau made sure that the ring received lucrative contracts and controlled the Indians' purchasing power. Government allotments were really payments to the Ring, with the Indians being just temporary moneyholders.

Under President Rutherford B. Hayes, Carl Schurz was appointed to the office of Secretary of the Interior. He was a strong ecologist and reformer who fought the Indian Ring for four years. One of his actions to protect the Indian was the appointment of strong men as agents, men who would not bend to the Ring's corruption. He selected Dr. McGillycuddy to assume the position of Indian agent at the Pine Ridge Reservation.

McGillycuddy increased rations to the Indians who had to travel the farthest to the post; he formed a reservation police force of 50 Indians; and he clashed with both redmen and whitemen to do what he believed was right for the reservation.

He was a friend of Young Man Afraid, who was the Chief of the Sioux. In one instance he gave the Chief permission to hunt buffalo in the north, sending the following press release to the Deadwood newspaper:

"Will you please give notice that Chief Young Man Afraid leaves here today with a party of 100 Oglalas for a buffalo hunt north of the hills. He is our best chief and I bespeak kind treatment for him and his party."

His clash was with an equally powerful Indian, Red Cloud, who was war chief and resented his loss of power on the reservation. McGillycuddy was the symbol of the new — schoolhouses, farms, laborers, freighters and beef. He had abolished the Sun Dance, and he did not recognize Red Cloud as chief. The two men became lifelong adversaries.

However, Dr. Bland, an Easterner, financed a publication called "Council Fire," which gave Red Cloud all the press exposure he could ask for; and the Indian Ring accused McGillycuddy of everything that it could in an effort to get an Indian Ring choice in as agent. Red Cloud threatened Dr. McGillycuddy — leave the reservation or be killed. Fort Robinson wanted to send troops, but the agent said, "No, my promise was not to call troops if Indians provided police."

In the Indian Council McGillycuddy asked whether he had been right in not sending for troops. The Indians assured him that he had been. They tried unsuccessfully to get Red Cloud to come to Council. McGillycuddy's next move was to call in his police and

ask them where they stood. Six Feathers said he could not fight Red Cloud, who was his kinsman, but the other 49 members stood behind the agent.

In the meantime, the Council sent Yellow Hair with the message to "come to Council or we turn our warriors over to the agent." Red Cloud replied, "The Great Spirit has deserted me. I will come."

But the personal war between Red Cloud and McGillycuddy was not over. In 1884, McGillycuddy was summoned to Washington to answer charges of abuse of office. On the way his wagon overturned; some of the Doctor's ribs were broken. At Fort Niobrara he was told to stay and get healed, but he replied, "I am going to be tried. How can I be tried if I am not there?"

In pain and irritation he appeared before the Indian Commission and told them that he would conduct his own case, as he could not afford to waste money "on a farce of this kind." When the Commissioner and his men took offense, McGillycuddy stated that he did not intend to cast aspersions on the Commissioner or his high office, but that he did intend to cast aspersions on a system which forced him to come fifteen-hundred miles to answer charges brought by the class of people before him.

He was willing to conduct his own case as soon as he was given a copy of the charges; but even at this late date, no charges had been written. The hearing had to be delayed.

Colonel Maypenny was the first witness against him, and he railed on about broken treaties and misconduct. At the end of that statement, McGillycuddy asked him if he had ever been to Pine Ridge or if he knew anything beyond what he had been told by others. The Colonel's answer was "No," and McGillycuddy rested.

On the stand McGillycuddy stood up to each and every charge against him, and the prosecutor brought up the final charge:

"You offered inducements to Young Man Afraid to set himself up as head chief of the Oglalas and thereby usurped the powers of Chief Red Cloud, did you not?"

McGillycuddy sat silently while Young Man Afraid rose from the floor, wrapped in a blue blanket adorned in beadwork and porcupine quills. A single eagle feather stood upright from his hair, and he spoke:

"As far as the memory of the Sioux nation reaches, my father and his father and his father before him have been chiefs of the Oglalas. I was born a chief; no one can make me one. I am Young Man of Whose Horse They Are Afraid, rightful chief of the Oglala Sioux. Is it not so, Red Cloud?"

Red Cloud was silent.

McGillycuddy's tests were not always bureaucratic or Indian in nature. The reservations also attracted men who were only on the edge of the law. Nick Janiss hung around the traders' store during the day to mix with the Indians and squawmen. On his way home he would walk past the agent's office. One day McGillycuddy watched as Nick approached; and when he walked by, the agent stepped out and swung into step beside him. As they walked, Vincent McGillycuddy spoke, "I have something to say to you, Nick. I have had it in my mind for some time, but I waited to make sure of my suspicions before doing so. You are stirring up mischief among the Indians and the half-breeds. You have some influence over them, not because you are a big man, but simply because Red Cloud's sister is your squaw. On that account you are carried on the payrolls and fed.

"You have been responsible for attacks on settlers and for many deaths on the borders. You've had your way long enough — don't reach for your gun, Nick — you'd be dead before you could get it."

The agent's hand was in his pocket, and Nick glanced at it nervously.

"You've got to give up your devilry, Nick, or you'll be ordered off the reservation. And if you're ordered off and don't stay off — well, that's all I have to say, Nick. I've given you warning. Good night."

Nick said nothing. He merely slouched away. As he disappeared, McGillycuddy withdrew his empty hand from his empty pocket, smiled, and walked back to his office.

His reservation days were filled with accusations, and he was finally relieved of duty when he refused to accept a new clerk. He went back to The Hills and settled in Rapid City, where he became the President of the Lakota Banking and Investment Company, Vice President of the Black Hills National Bank, and organizer of the hydroelectric and power company.

He was called in as a consultant when the Ghost Dances began; but his advice, which was to leave the dances alone, was ignored. He maintained many of his Indian friends even after leaving the reservation. The panic of 1893 ruined his bank and his finances, but he continued to succeed. He then became President of the School of Mines and medical inspector for the Mutual Life Insurance Company.

His pathway wound to California after his wife suffered a stroke. There he was approached by a chorus girl who sat on his lap and asked Mrs. McGillycuddy, "If you die, would you mind if I married Mr. McGillycuddy?" After his wife's death, the unlikely question became fact. He married the chorus girl and lived out the remainder of his life with her.

Dr. Vincent McGillycuddy never came back to The Hills, but his ashes did. The box containing his cremated remains was placed on top of Harney Peak. His strand of the web was complete.

The web of the Black Hills reached to the Big Horns, up and around the curve of the Missouri, and across the Platte River. It was part of the Bad Lands, the grasslands, and the wild west. The web included Indians and fortune seekers. Life in one location would send its vibrations throughout the whole. What happened in the Black Hills affected the people of Pierre, Medora, Bismarck, Cheyenne, and Sidney.

CHAPTER 2 # THE BADLANDS

As I climbed up the back side of a steep ridge, I thought of the Ranger's words, "You can't get where you're going from where you're starting." Inwardly I laughed; and as I reached the summit, a narrow neck of grey bentonite draped over red and tan siltstone, and peered into the maze ahead, I was surprised to see one ridge peering back.

On another dome a bighorn stood, transfixed, almost stunned at the interloper he saw. Then another joined him, and still another, and the troop grew to thirteen, strung out from the dome along a narrow ridge and finally down into another chasm. This was the heart of the Pinnacles, the fantasyland of the White River and the middle of the Badlands National Park.

A small gulley grew into a steep valley that meandered between crumbling walls and then became a delta of clay between the Pinnacles. Rubber rabbit bush and gumweed flower were buttons of yellow in the grey landscape, and signs of human disturbance were very few. This was The Badlands; Mako Sica; Les Mavaises Terres A'Traverser.

Annie Tallent, the first white woman in the Black Hills, wrote: ". . . Language is inadequate to describe the utter desolation of the country through which we passed. Long ranges of hills, cut up by a perfect labyrinth of ravines or gorges into all sorts of fantastic shapes, into various architectural forms, resembling fortresses, castles, and even small villages, confronted us on every hand . . . I felt convinced that no human being could long abide in such a place.

The raw wood of a wind-stripped fencepost and the sagging barbed wire, hanging down where no man had been in years, tried to mark sections of earth in neat little squares, but the clay butte had moved at its own whim, never knowing it had been owned.

The creek became bisected and trisected as tributaries disappeared up the precipitous side walls. A new streambed replaced the original and moved upward, gradually and steadily getting smaller until it disappeared at the base of a sandstone cliff. The air was pungent with the scent of sage, and shriveled pieces of clay rested on the slopes like ballbearings. From this point the Badlands sprawled like a

multi-legged earth monster, each leg being a different variation on the bad land's theme.

Beneath the rim of a square-edged butte above Sage Creek one hundred bison grazed and dusted themselves in a prairie dog town. On a plateau above the Big White River, bighorns grazed on a tabletop while the setting sun made a color display on the striped buttes in the distance.

Here in the Pinnacles the sun danced between the sky-scratching peaks; and shadows formed, moved, and disappeared as though a thousand shadowy figures lurked in the sandstone wall. John Muir called Yosemite the "Valley of Light," but the Badlands have to be called the land of sunsets, sunrises, and shadows.

Teddy Roosevelt wrote:

The grassy, scantily wooded bottoms through which the winding river flows are bounded by bare, jagged buttes; their fantastic shapes and sharp, steep edges throw the most curious shadows, under the cloudless sky; and at evening I love to sit out in front of the hut and see their hard gray outlines gradually growing soft and purple as the flaming sunset by degrees softens . . .

The Badlands appear to be hills, but actually they are remnants of the land. The Badlands are a valley, not a ridge. When the Black Hills rose and the Rocky Mountains buckled, streams buried the old swamplands with river deltas. Then, as the land continued to rise and the streams moved faster, the waters eroded the land rather than burying it. South Dakota was divided into prairie and mountains, with an obstacle between. The obstacle — the wall — became a landmark.

A bone stuck out from the mud. It was a fossilized, rock-hard bone of some ancient creature that had come here because of the abundance of water — an animal that roamed swamps and lowlands rather than sunbaked ridges. Even Annie Tallent, in her memoirs, called this the land of the scientists. Animals with tongue-knotting names like titanothere and oreodont were common in the years called Oligocene and Miocene. Here were early forms of camel, sabre-toothed cat and rhinoceros. Jawbones and skulls with teeth that had tasted kinds of animals that no longer even exist were partially exposed above the yellow rock region. A tortoise shell, smooth and elliptical, lay partially exposed to the sun.

Fossils aren't the only bones of the prairies. Death is as much a part of the prairie as life, and pronghorn bones drying and fading in the sun are not uncommon sights. Two pronghorns bounded out of sight, a reminder of prairie abundance and of the herd of 35,000,000 that roamed these plains in the 1880's.

A prairie dog town stood in the path and seemed rather docile, except for a few barking dogs on the perimeter, but the barking was soon replaced by a high-pitched buzzing. The whine, the incessant droning sound encircled me and tapped my pores, searching for blood. The air blackened with mosquitoes, and I could rub my hands down each leg and back up, killing a hundred animals with each stroke. I felt nauseous, the winds blew, the sun glared down, and the prairie dog mosquitoes kept coming.

Beyond the prairie dog town a brown spectre loomed and broke the spell of dusk as it carved a swath through the sky. A golden striped head and yellow talons stood out amidst the six-foot wingspan, leaving everything stunned. Perhaps it is in this dramatic fashion that the golden eagle hypnotizes its prey. His flight curved up, and the bird disappeared into the twilight above the Pinnacles.

The land below the sandstone spines, where streams run broken-field patterns until they meet and rush off to the west, that appeared to be flat from a distance dropped off into ten-foot canyons. The field is a mosaic of tables, grassy on top with prickly pear edges and grey-brown sides. The choice is to climb in and out of each stream bed or choose one and meander with it.

Dusk set in, and I spread a ground cloth on the smooth outwash from the ridges, opened my supply of jerky and mixture of seeds and dried fruit, and relaxed as the twilight lengthened the surrounding silhouettes, causing them to assume grotesque gnome-like features.

The wind played in the ravines, carrying small particles to sting face and hands. Winds are a part of the land; when they cease, I expect the bison and mule deer to fall over, for they must constantly lean into them. The winds move seeds and scents and sands and storms.

The wind blew towering thunderheads around the sky like fluffy billiard balls, and the sky between turned yellow with warning. Cracks of lightning split the horizon, and rumbles of thunder shook the earth beneath my feet. On the butte tops coyotes wailed and seemed to be comforting each other.

All night the thunder roared and the wind blew. Even though it was late July, the thermometer plunged into the 40's overnight and climbed very little during the next day. The grey skies gave the appearance of autumn, and my mind pictured an October day when the constant flapping of the tentfly was punctuated with sharper, honking sounds. The wind-swept grasslands and the greyness of the sky seemed to flow into the land. There was no delineation between earth and sky — no sharpness, no contrast. The geese appeared like solidified droplets in this earth-sky fog, and then disappeared in the south like an ancient winged arrowhead. They were adventurers looking for jewels of water in a land of hidden riches.

Over the rise and onto the hump of the Pinnacles the erosion spread in all directions, but the landscape on top was different. There were soft domes and a dike of ash that stood like an ancient ruin amongst the clay. It was three inches thick and six feet tall at the biggest spot, but mostly it was a doll-sized Great Wall of China and another bizarre part of this country.

My back was to the Pinnacles now, and I moved towards Sage Creek Basin. Water actually filled part of the stream bed, and I thought of the paradox that this land presented — hot, dry, sparse, yet built up by water deposit and torn down by water erosion.

Animal tracks were in the mud, telling tales about the animal and the paradoxes that abound here. False impressions or poor perceptions, it doesn't matter. The games of the mind are part of the fun of being out. Red-winged blackbirds bantered with their "con-cur-reee" song, a paradox again! Here in the land of the lazuli bunting, lark bunting, sharp-tailed grouse, and meadowlark, the red-wings are out of place.

On the other side of a knoll lay an oasis, a pond ringed in cottonwood and sedge. The birds were ecstatic about their nest, a frog bounded into the water, and tracks of bison and deer dotted the muddy shore. Behind the pond was a sculptured fin of earth, dry and ponderous, scratching the sky.

I sipped and munched in the sun as a red striped prairie garter snake moved from beside me. Earlier that month I had walked another part of the Badlands and had found four prairie rattlers. They were all shy and unassuming animals who anxiously moved away from my big feet.

In one spot there was a startling slap, like a slab of beef on a butcher's counter. In a saddle of smooth clay between two humps of earth two rattlesnakes body-wrestled, their own unique variation of arm wrestling. They raised their front halves, intertwining and swaying back and forth in a hypnotizing dance, until one head rose over the other and the snake that had gained an advantage drove its adversary to the ground, pinning it momentarily. Then they both dispersed. The sound had been a preliminary takedown, but there had been no pin. These primitive animals have developed a non-lethal combat to determine territory. Rather than biting and killing each other, they wrestle.

I ascended through the yellow and the red layers and up the steep banks of the wall where I had glided so enjoyably on crosscountry skis in the winter. The seasonal mosaic became a part of the sweep of the vista. Bison fringed with snow, their breath a cloud on the horizon; green grasses in the spring; reddish cone flowers peering through the grasses of summer; and the orange glow of turkeyfoot aging gracefully in the prairie year are all accurate images of this spot.

Near the road prairie dogs scolded instamatic tourists while two burrowing owls stood, unnoticed, in the back of the town. People milled and buzzed and then ran back to their air-conditioned vehicles.

Dusty and thirsty, I walked past tourists who were too hurried to walk down the hill. Someone said, "This land really is worthless," and I knew that they were saying what was expected of them.

Lame Deer said, "We are a part of the Nature around us, and the older we get, the more we come to look like it. In the end we become part of the landscape with a face like the Badlands."

CHAPTER 3 THE GRASSLAND INDIANS

When Custer's expedition went in search of gold, they expected to find an armed Indian fortress in the Black Hills. Warren's earlier movement into Indian territory was also a tactical mission to learn the strength of the Indian stronghold, but the Black Hills were the Indians' temple of worship, a storehouse of God that was not meant to be a home.

The Hills were a wilderness preserve of the American Indian. Indians came here for tipi poles, water, game, and worship, but they did not stay here.

To understand the Black Hills a person must walk the grasslands. The Badlands are dramatic in their starkness, and The Hills are massive and bold against the skyline.

Life was on the prairies where pronghorn and buffalo roamed. The bison were more than an animal of the plains, they were a lifestyle in themselves. They offered meat and blanket, bone tools, tipi covers, medicine, and part of religion. The great seas of grass provided sustenance for the inland warrior, and the multitudinous herds had the potential to support a great Indian nation. But to take advantage of the bounty, the Indian required one more animal.

The horse was a reintroduction of a North American animal. The Spaniards, who ran rampant over so many Indian cultures, did not realize that they brought the animal that would enable the North American Indian to rise to new heights.

The horse had not been in the United States since its bones had fossilized in the Badlands. The same land bridge that led men to North America led the horse to Asia.

Without the horse, the plains Indian lived along riverways on the fringe of the great prairies, growing crops and practicing the arts of pottery and weaving. They were subjected to the whims of flood and drought, and survival was a constant occupation.

Before the arrival of the horse, bison were driven over cliffs in wild stampedes or they were stalked on snowshoes and were ambushed. Now a mounted rider could go into the midst of a buffalo herd. The buffalo hunters could move freely on the backs of their "sunka wakan," meaning mysterious dog. The bison and the horse were the Sioux Indian, and the mounted Indian would be the symbol of the grasslands.

The plains Indian was so closely allied to the horse that in some tribes it was the custom for mothers to tie their son's umbilical cord to the tail or mane of their favorite pony. Horse songs were sung, horses were given as marriage gifts, and horses were killed to give the dead owner a means of riding into the other world.

The Sioux were not the first to live in this land; in fact, they were the last of the prairie nations. There were Kiowa, Cheyenne, Mandan, Arikara, Pawnee, Crow, and Gross Ventres before them. These early agricultural tribes were compact societies that were susceptible to white men's diseases. Their very location insured them of meeting the first white explorers and exploiters who would use the nation's river highways. They were strong people who could face blizzards, drought, near starvation, thirst, and suffering; but they had not developed a resistance to diseases that they had never encountered before. Smallpox, cholera, and measles decimated their nations.

The more nomadic Cheyenne may have rivaled the Sioux as prairie knights, but they lost a third of their tribe to cholera in 1849 and lost the remainder of their nation in the Sand Creek Massacre of 1864, the Battle of Washita in 1868, and in Mackenzie's raids of 1877.

Each of these tribes was a rival and a shareholder of the prairie. They fought and parried with one another for decades, but their demise left only one strong tribe. The Dakota formed a confederacy of seven tribes — the seven council fires. These included three main groups: the Santee, consisting of Medwakanten, Sisseton, Wanpekut and Wahpeton, in Minnesota; the Teton Dakotas, including Oglala, Brule, Hunkpapa, Miniconjou, Two Kettle, Sansarc, and Sihasapa, who moved into the plains in the 1700's; and the Yankton Sioux in eastern South Dakota.

Like three large dominoes, the divisions of the Sioux nation lined up across Minnesota and South Dakota, and their interactions with white culture in the east had repercussions throughout the west. The Sioux were not considered to be good trade partners for the French Canadians, but the Cree and the Ojibwa received guns in trade with the voyageurs and they turned their guns on their old enemies, the Nadowessioux (serpents). Underpowered, the Sioux could not stave off the aggression of their old rivals. Their days in the woods were limited.

The woodland Sioux were driven by the Ojibwa, but they were cornered by the white men. In a reservation along the Minnesota River they were no longer people of the wild rice, deer, bear, and moose. They were to be farmers and welfare recipients. Their lifestyle was taken; their freedom removed. They were expected to wait for government checks and government beef and to listen to the wisdom of Indian agents and white store owners. There was tension all throughout the land, and it broke with the killing of a farmer over the theft of some chickens.

A nation in civil war was now in a race war.

The Sioux moved west to the Dakotas, pursued by the military. Near Sioux Falls, a fugitive chief, Little Crow, sat around a council fire with western Sioux, including then unknown Sitting Bull. The chiefs knew defeat was inevitable, but they also knew the times and the needs of their people. They knew justice was not available to them, and they needed dignity more than handouts. Territory for the Sioux in Minnesota was all but gone. A few Sioux tribes held on, some Sioux were hung, and others moved west. Pressures continued to mount for the Dakota Indian.

Shortly after the 1862 uprising, Red Cloud fought a war along the Powder River which the Indians won, their only major success. The wave of new settlers was slowed. Forts were torn down. The post-Civil War military had to back up a step. It was the height of Sioux supremacy on the plains. Their territory was well defined and livable. They were the greatest light cavalry in the world.

Hunting time diminished, and success increased. There was leisure time for ceremonies and stories, and the culture of the Sioux flourished. The Indians could now engage in trade; that brought more of them to the Black Hills region.

Great leaders emerged. Religion took new definition. But the buffalo herd continued to dwindle, and that strained their lifestyle. White men wanted to rewrite treaties and digest more Indian lands.

There were settlers in North Dakota, eastern South Dakota, and Nebraska. The Oregon Trail was crisscrossed by other trails, and the Civil War had left a nation with a surplus of field generals but no battles to be fought. The prairies were about to turn red with the blood of bison and men, and the prize would be the Black Hills.

CHAPTER 4

FORT MEADE

At Fort Meade Military Cemetery, on the edge of the Black Hills, one can look at two gravemarkers that read "Child of Civilian Refugee" and "Lucy, Child, Sioux Indian" and view the sacred Bear Butte in the distance. In this cemetery is the grave of William Fool Soldier, who was a Teton Sioux who had been traded for a white woman in order to release her. The Indians who engaged in this swap were called "Fool Soldiers" since they received nothing for their efforts.

Buried here are a native of Scotland, a Prussian, a pioneer woman who lived to be 80, and many members of the 25th Infantry — a troop of black soldiers.

No doubt the reasons for this Indian war are represented right here at Fort Meade. Its boundaries went right up to the base of the sacred mountain and the soldier's job was to protect citizens of the United States who were stealing Indian land. The frustration and justifications for the Indians are apparent.

The Cavalry justification will probably be found in the words scratched in sandstone by Ezra Kind:

Came to these hills in 1833, seven of us DeLacompt Ezra Kind G.W. Wood T Brown R Kent Wm King Indian Crow, all ded but me Ezra Kind. Killed by Inds beyond the high hill got our gold June 1834.

On the back of the stone he had written:

Got all of the gold we could carry our pony all got by the Indians. I have lost my gun and nothing to eat and Indians hunting me.

Perhaps the sentiment of the time was even better expressed by Annie Tallent when she wrote:

In 1874 the campfires of the red man were extinguished in the Black Hills, never again to be rekindled. The spirit of adventure and aggression was then abroad in the land; the handwriting was on the wall. The gold-ribbed Black Hills were to be snatched from the grasp of savages, to whom they were no longer profitable even as the hunting ground, and given over to the thrift and enterprise of the hardy pioneer, who would develop their wonderful resources and thereby advance the interests and add to the wealth of our whole country.

War was inevitable. Manifest destiny was a disease that the nation was afflicted with.

The troops were primarily black and Irish, the two ethnic groups that suffered the greatest prejudices in the United States. Maybe the cavalry was their only escape from this hatred. If it was, it was an incomplete escape. The blacks, which the Indians called Buffalo Soldiers, always had white officers; in the eyes of the War Department, they were not capable of commanding positions.

For the soldiers at Fort Meade, the nearby town of Sturgis was their only relief from boredom. If they didn't get respect there, they could certainly get plenty of action.

Tallent wrote:

According to its own confession it has frequently presented scenes of mad recklessness that outrivaled in lawlessness even the worst days of the early mining camps of the Hills. These conditions were occasioned in good part by the riotous behavior of the colored infantry men, who garrisoned Fort Meade at the time. Whisky flowed like water, and whenever they visited the town, on leave of absence, after imbibing copious draughts of the fiery fluid, they proceeded to paint Main street in all sorts of lurid colors, as if they were its sole proprietors.

Frequent collisions occurred between these black soldiers and the allround white toughs who sometimes inflicted their unwelcome presence upon the community, resulting in black eyes, cut faces, and bruised anatomies generally.

Is it any wonder that these men looked for a reason to fight and often initiated minor skirmishes? They were hired to fight and forced to sit. To make life easier, glee clubs and bands were formed.

Life for the Indian was much different. Chief Flying Hawk, an Oglala, described the benefit of the tipi:

The Tipi is much better to live in; always clean, warm in winter, cool in summer; easy to move. The white man builds big house, cost much money, like big cage, shut out sun, can never move; always sick. Indians and animals know better how to live than white man; nobody can be in good health if he does not have all the time fresh air, sunshine and good water. If the Great Spirit wanted men to stay in one place he would make the world stand still; but He made it to always change, so birds and animals can move and always have green grass and ripe berries, sunlight to work and play, and night to sleep; summer for flowers to bloom, and winter for them to sleep; always changing; everything for good; nothing for nothing.

The white man does not obey the Great Spirit; that is why the Indians never could agree with him.

Fort Lincoln, Fort Randall, Fort Sully, Fort Meade, Fort Laramie, and Fort Robinson made a ring of fortresses around the tipis. The Hills were being ripped apart to uncover yellow metal, and the Indian was being squeezed from within and without.

The leaders of the Indian wars of the plains were the "Who's Who" of the western military. There were Sherman, Sheridan, Custer, Terry, Miles, and Crook on one side, and Red Cloud, Sitting Bull, Crazy Horse, Gall, Spotted Tail, and American Horse on the other. These were men of stature, and they spoke their frustrations.

Red Cloud: When we first had this land we were strong; now we are melting like snow on a hillside, while you are grown like spring grass. Now, I have come a long distance to my Great Father's House. See if I have left any blood in his land when I go. When the white man comes to my country he leaves a trail of blood behind him. . . .

I have two mountains in that country. The Black Hills and the Big Horn Mountain. I want the Father to make no roads through them. I have told these things three times and now I have come to tell them the fourth. I do not want my reservation on the Missouri. This is the fourth time I have said so. . . ."

Sheridan: We took away their country, broke up their mode of living, their habits of life, introduced disease and decay among them, and it was for this and against this that they made war. Could anyone expect less?

Crazy Horse: We did not ask you white men to come here. The Great Spirit gave us this country as a home. You had yours. We did not interfere with you. The Great Spirit gave us plenty of land to live on, and buffalo, deer, antelope and other game. But you have come here; you are taking my land from me; you are killing off our game, so it is hard for us to live. Now, you tell us to work for a living, but the Great Spirit did not make us to work, but to live by hunting. You white men can work if you want to. We do not interfere with you, and again you say, why do you not become civilized? We do not want your civilization! We would live as our fathers did, and their fathers before them.

Sheridan: The only good Indian is a dead Indian.

Sitting Bull: Behold, my brothers, the spring has come; the earth has received the embraces of the sun and we shall soon see the results of that love!

Every seed is awakened and so has all animal life. It is through this mysterious power that we too have our being and we therefore yield to our neighbors, even our animal neighbors, the same right as ourselves, to inhabit this land.

Yet, hear me, people, we have now to deal with another race — small and feeble when our fathers first met them but now great and overbearing. Strangely enough they have a mind to till the soil and the love of possession is a disease with them. These people have made many rules that the rich may break but the poor may not. They take tithes from the poor and weak to support the rich who rule. They claim this mother of ours, the earth, for their own and fence their neighbors away; they deface her with their buildings and their refuse. That nation is like a spring freshet that overruns its banks and destroys all who are in its path.

We cannot dwell side by side. Only seven years ago we made a treaty by which we were assured that the buffalo country should be left to us forever. Now they threaten to take that away from us. My brothers, shall we submit or shall we say to them: 'First kill me before you take possession of my Fatherland'. . . .

Sherman: We must act with vindictive earnestness against the Sioux, even to their extermination, men, women and children.

Spotted Tail: This war did not spring up here in our land; this war was brought upon us by the children of the Great Father who came to take our land from us without price, and who, in our land, do a great many evil things. The Great Father and his children are to blame for this trouble. . . . It has been our wish to live here in our country peaceable, and do such things as may be for the welfare and good of our people, but the Great Father has filled it with soldiers who think only of our death.

Sheridan: These men (buffalo hunters) have done in the last two years, and will do in the next year, more to settle the vexed Indian question than the entire regular army has done in the last thirty years. They are destroying the Indians' commissary; and it is a well-known fact that an army losing its base of supplies is placed at a great disadvantage. Send them powder and lead, if you will; but for the sake of a lasting peace, let them kill, skin and sell until the buffaloes are exterminated. Then your prairies can be covered with speckled cattle and the festive cowboy, who follows the hunter as a second forerunner of an advanced civilization.

Sitting Bull: Our rations have been reduced to almost nothing, and many of our people have starved to death. Now I beg you to have the amount of our rations increased so our children will not starve. . . .I want clothing, too. . . .We want some clothing this month, and when it gets cold we want more to protect us from the weather. That is all I have to say.

Crook: if our aim be to remove the aborigine from a state of servile independence, we cannot begin in a better or more practical way than by making him think well of himself, to force upon him the knowledge that he is part and parcel of the nation, clothed with all its political privileges, entitled to share in all its benefits. Our present treatment degrades him in his own eyes. . . .

The real symbol of this bitterness was General George Armstrong Custer. He was the flamboyant boy general, hero to the Black Hills inhabitants, showman, and egotist. He marched his men from Fort Lincoln near Bismarck to search for gold in the Black Hills in almost Hollywood style. There were glee clubs and bands, a female black cook, and even champagne. Custer liked ceremony and status, and even the horses were distributed by color to show off rank.

Custer became the victim in the largest and single most important battle of the Indian wars. When he rode over the grassy hills of the Little Big Horn River into the largest Indian force the world has ever seen, he went beyond his orders. First, he refused to wait for General Terry and General Gibbon to arrive, and then he divided his troops into three forces with expectations that he could march triumphantly through the Indian encampment without aid. He was out of favor in Washington, and he wanted to do something spectacular to regain his fame.

What he did was destroy the Indian nation with his death. The Indian won too easily, too decisively, and the defeat of a hero caused passions to soar. All other reasons to fight were too hard to reconcile. Manifest destiny was congressional catch-all that it meant nothing to the soldier, but Custer and his troops were buddies. Each soldier knew the feeling of Custer on that little knoll. They could understand the helpless feeling of the troopers who were surrounded by the Indian nation.

The soldiers heard stories of mutilated bodies on the battlefield. The frontier fighter didn't want to get captured, for that meant torture. They were determined fighters. No one questioned Custer's right to take his men into battle, nor his willingness to sacrifice their lives for his glory.

It was accepted, just as General Crook's men accepted the mud march and the near starvation that came with the battle of Slim Buttes to the north of the Black Hills. They were expected to fight and to suffer. Their health was their own problem, and all the military gave them was a post surgeon and a page of health rules.

"TAKE CARE OF YOUR HEALTH" The following extract of advice to soldiers are from Dr. Hall and others:

1. In any ordinary campaign, sickness disables or destroys three times as many as the sword.

2. Sunstroke may be prevented by wearing a silk handkerchief in the crown of the hat, by a wet cloth, or by moistened green leaves or grass.

3. Never lie or sit down on the grass or bare earth for a moment; rather use your hat: a handkerchief, even, is a protection. The warmer you are, the greater need for precaution, as a damp vapor is immediately generated, to be absorbed by the clothing, and to cool you off too rapidly.

War was a giant game played by professional strategists and politicians, and it had its own rules of conduct. The Indian counted coup. They got honor points for capturing an enemy's ceremonial pipe, war shirt, war bonnet, shield, or bow. They also were recognized for scalps and the capture of an enemy's horse, but the most complicated form of tribute was found in the coup stick.

Wars between Indian tribes were ritualistic. Death was a part of the battle, but that only added honor to the other parts of the warfare. Unarmed warriors would ride into a battle to touch the enemy with a stick, not to kill them, for a feather was often the only armament on the stick. It was a battlefield form of tag.

When red men fought white and black men, the coup stick seemed ridiculous to the cavalry man. It is hard to tag and run when the enemy can tag back with a bullet, but then the U.S. military had its own coup takers.

The town of Sturgis still bears the name of the first military camp. Lieutenant Sturgis was a member of Custer's battalion at the Little Big Horn, and his father was the first post commander.

The "Star Spangled Banner" was played at all military functions at Fort Meade, a practice nowhere else at that time. The Fort was playing it 39 years before it was declared the national anthem. On that parade ground Sheridan, sword in hand, pointed out the location of the future fort buildings from the back of his cavalry mount. To the east was a stable, the home of Commanche, and to the north were the quarters of Major Reno. Both of these figures had been at the Little Big Horn and their lives at Fort Meade would be the last two scenarios in the Custer epic.

At the Big Horn Battle in 1876 Custer divided his forces into four commands: he had five troops, Major Reno had three, Captain McDougal had one, and Captain Benteen had three. Charley Reynolds, one of the most respected scouts in military history, warned Custer that it was "the biggest bunch of Indians I have ever seen." Captain Benteen was sent south; in effect, he was being removed from the action. Major Reno was sent to one end of the encampment, and Captain McDougal was to try to keep up with the ammunition packs.

Benteen asked, "Hadn't we better keep the regiment together? If that is a big camp, we will need every man we have."

Custer replied, "You have your orders. Sound to horse."

The scouts entrusted their valuables to troopers in Reno's and Benteen's commands and prepared to die. Only Custer refused to see the future.

Reno attacked and fell back under siege. Custer was surrounded. His troops were massacred. Benteen found Reno, who had refused to go toward Custer without ammunition, and the forces joined on a hilltop to ward off the Indian advance. Reno and his officers were excited, mad, and bewildered. Benteen took command.

The men were trapped and at the Indian's mercy, but the Indians broke camp and moved on. Sustained battle was not the Indian technique. Maybe the Indians were tired of the fight. Maybe they felt that Sitting

Bull's vision had been fulfilled already. Or perhaps they knew that Terry and Gibbon were coming with the troops that Custer was supposed to have met before engaging the Sioux.

The survivors were quick to look for Custer and his men. What they found was a grisly scene of death and mutilation. Everything was dead, except for one horse — Commanche, who became a symbol, a rallying point to be treated unlike any other horse in the military. By special orders he was to receive care and good pasture at Fort Meade. He lived there twelve years.

Major Reno was also assigned to Fort Meade, but not for special care. Reno was the center of bitter controversy. He was criticized for not going to Custer's aid, and he was held responsible for Custer's death by many. Even the court's vindication of his actions did not take away the suspicions and bitterness.

Reno's career in the military had not been one of great glories. It took him three tries to graduate from West Point, 20th in a class of 38. He was suspended twice. The incoming freshmen that year included George Armstrong Custer, who would graduate four years later, last in a class of 34.

In 1873 Reno had been assigned to Fort Abraham Lincoln, Custer's command, on the banks of the Missouri River near the site of Mandan, North Dakota. During the time Reno was stationed there, Custer was involved with the Black Hills' expedition and the investigations of Grant's generals in Washington. Reno worried about the protection of Northern Pacific Railroad workers in North Dakota and escorted the Northern Boundary Survey Commission from Lake of the Woods to the Rocky Mountains.

Reno's wife died while he was in Montana. When he applied for a leave, he was refused permission by General Terry. From this incident he turned to the bottle for support. His career went continually downhill. His next adventure was at the Little Big Horn in August, 1876.

In December, 1876, Major Reno took command of Fort Abercrombie, North Dakota; and on February 28, 1877, he was subjected to a nine-day court martial at St. Paul. Two charges were brought against him. The first stated that he had taken improper liberties with Captain Bell's wife and in seven specific instances it charged Reno with "taking both her hands in his own, and attempting to draw her person to his own," and after his unsuccessful advances, he chose to defame her character. The second charge stated that he had bribed a black servant to testify in Reno's behalf.

Reno was found guilty of six of the seven parts of the first charge, and not guilty of the second charge. He was dismissed, and his military career should have been over; but President Hayes commuted the sentence to suspension from pay and rank for two years.

The day of the commuted sentence, Lieutenant Robinson filed new charges. In five charges Major Reno was accused of drunkenness and fighting at Fort Lincoln and Fort Abercrombie while in a position of command. Colonel Sturgis disapproved of these charges being leveled eight months after the fact, and his disapproval was supported by the War Department. The charges were dropped.

Then, Frederick Whittaker, with the help of Mrs. Custer, published a biography of Custer. In it he charged Reno with cowardice and disobedience on the battlefield. He also accused both Reno and Benteen of willful neglect.

Major Reno asked the President for a court of inquiry into this matter. The request was granted. After 26 days the inquiry concluded with the statement: "The conduct of the officers throughout was excellent and while subordinates in some instances did more for the safety of the command by brilliant displays of courage than did Major Reno, there was nothing in his conduct which requires animadversion (censure) from this court."

Suspension and suspicion were supposed to end when he reported to Fort Meade on May 21, 1879, but four months later he faced another court martial on three charges: assault of a Second Lieutenant over a gambling debt, drunk and disorderly conduct in a public saloon, and intoxication at the residence of the post trader.

While awaiting trial, the troubled Major added to his woes, and a last charge was added. Major Reno "did in the darkness and at a late hour in the evening, surreptitiously enter the side grounds adjoining the private residence of quarters of his commanding officer, Colonel S. D. Sturgis, 7th Cavalry, and did peer into a side window of the family sitting room of said residence or quarters, approaching so near and so stealthily as to very seriously affright and alarm that portion of the family of the said Colonel S. D. Sturgis, 7th Cavalry, which had not yet retired for the night, and were still below stairs and occupants of said family sitting room."

The question of Major Reno's visit to the window brought many uncomfortable and inflamed moments to the court, but Captain Benteen, his compatriot commander at the massacre, may have given the clearest picture of the events when he testified, "I mean by this that he did not express all that he meant and felt, that he was dead in love with the young lady was my belief."

The court found Reno guilty of each of the three actions in the first charge, but not guilty of the charge itself. He was found guilty of a substitute charge which did not require dismissal.

The fourth and final charge was the one that got the Major. It found him not guilty of "very seriously" alarming the occupants, but guilty of the rest of the charge. Then five judges signed a statement to the record asking the confirming authority to have leniency on the Major. The wishy-washy case then went to the War Department.

Major Reno asked for the right to resign. When he found out that five of seven judges asked for clemency, he withdrew his request. That was a mistake, for Major Reno lost.

General Terry, Department Commander, wrote:

The sentence is manifestly excessive as a punishment for the acts of which Major Reno was found guilty under the first charge and its specifications. But as I have no powers to modify it, and as my disapproval of it would put an end to the case, leaving Reno without any punishment whatever, I formally approve it. I join, however, in the recommendation of a majority of the members of the court, that it be modified.

General Sherman asked the sentence to be changed to suspension, and a judge advocate suggested a transfer. President Hayes took in the reports and acted on a court martial of Major Reno for the second time in two years. He confirmed the sentence.

Major Reno was dismissed on April 1, 1880. He died of pneumonia and cancer in 1889. In 1967 his court martial was overturned, and he was reburied in the cemetery at the Little Big Horn.

CHAPTER 5 # THE SKY PILLARS

BEAR BUTTE

The buttress of talus and lava rises like a column from the ground. Bear Butte, the site of Custer's grizzly bear kill, was the landmark of the Pierre Deadwood Trail and the Bismarck Deadwood Trail. It was the summit from which the Indian could watch the ants of emigration march to plunder his home. But most important, it was a temple, a sacred shrine. Here were mingled the spirits of the Mandan, the Sioux, and the Cheyenne. This was the place of visions, of cleansing of the spirit, and of enlightenment.

The Cheyenne tell of Sweet Medicine, the young brave who murdered an elder over a disputed bison kill and was banished from his tribe, who then came to Bear Butte and met a banished maiden. Together they lived on the mountain for four years and then were invited to a cave inhabited by gods.

"We present you with two bundles. Which do you take?"

The bundles each held four sacred arrows, one bundle having eagle feathers; the other, hawk. Both bundles had two dark war arrows and two light hunt and peace arrows. Sweet Medicine chose the arrows with eagle feathers, for eagles fly farther and are stronger.

The gods then gave four commandments. They forbade adultery, killing, stealing, and marriage within a person's own family. Sweet Medicine was to stay on the mountain for four more years and then share his wisdom with his nation.

At the end of his exile he shared the commandments and warned of fur-faced foreigners who would travel on fast animals and would teach the Indians to eat food and drink that would soften them.

It was on Bear Butte that the Oglala Chief Bear died in hand-to-hand combat with his namesake, and the Sioux would call the place Mato Paha in his memory.

Legends and images have always been part of the mystique of the butte. For the Mandans, this was the place where their canoe was saved in the big flood. The voyageurs painted another image when they called the monolith "the mountain of the horse Indians," for their first observation included Sioux racing their horses around the mountain's flanks.

Each vision and story are still in and on Bear Butte. The Cheyenne believe that everything that has ever happened in a place is still part of the present. All time flows together. All things that happen make the world what it is today. It is the story of ecology — cycling and recycling, and we shall be a part of the future as the past is part of us.

In the Sioux language there is no word for time as we know it. When it is convenient to do something, that is the time. Otherwise, time has no meaning.

The Indian still comes to Bear Butte, the sacred mountain, for four days of fasting and prayer. Prayer cloths are spread on the ground and symbolize the universe. A rock is placed in the middle, and by this the Indian has defined the limits of his world.

This was sacred ground, and I didn't want to tread; but the peak beckoned the way tall places and endless vistas do, and I knew that I must go to it. A soul tug-of-war went on inside me, and I stood on the bear's shoulder in a valley of grass and looked to the north.

A kestrel flew by, and swallows chattered. Then a prairie falcon came like a phantom from the pines, looped overhead, and darted west. My eyes followed, and he led them to two golden eagles, soaring in tandem, one over the other.

I watched their grace and strength and heard the calls of white-winged youths that fluttered into trees and on the ground. They were the sign, the precursor of a vision; one could walk and soar at once. My feet moved up the mountain, my soul floated above it.

Then, the vision took hold. This was a sky pillar — so were Devils Tower, Inyan Kara, and Harney Peak. My mind took off to other rocks that held the sky above the earth.

DEVILS TOWER

The big rocks are bold and special in a land of high places. Devils Tower is another cornerpost, its fluted columns jutting above the soft sandstones like a giant thimble. Phonolite is the name geologists give this rock. It has a message in it, and it has an aura to it.

At the right time the sun sits behind the Tower, and its light cascades over and around the peak like a halo. Pigeons careen from the ledges in precision drills, and a prairie falcon is a silhouette of grace and speed as it soars from the top. Vultures ride the thermals of the surrounding land, and the rock is a control tower for aerial displays. Deer romp in the woods on the flanks of the Tower, and beneath it prairie dogs bask in the sun.

A special tree grows on the southeast slope of the Tower's shoulders and sends roots between layers of sandstone. Day by day, year by year, the roots grow. Pressure is constant and unflagging, and slowly the rock is opening like a giant, limestone clam shell.

The Kiowa Indians called the Tower "mateo tepee," Grizzly Bear Lodge. Now we call the mountains east of the Tower the Bear Lodge Mountains. Evidently there were other images and legends to this place, for Colonel Dodge named this "Devils Tower" because he said the Indians called it "the bad god's tower."

There is a desire to climb this rock, to see its top, to touch the sky. Thousands have made the ascent. They have touched the rock beyond the bear claw marks where Ursa Major and Ursa Minor are the only bruins that can roam.

Partway up the Tower, beyond the tops of the ponderosa pine, where the eye can sweep the panorama of the Black Mountains, one can look toward Bear Butte or Inyan Kara. The Belle Fourche River meanders through the red cliffs below and disappears into sagebrush flats.

On one side of the Tower William Rogers built a wooden ladder. This now decaying set of wooden steps was part of a 350-foot ladder made of oak, ash, and willow. Each step was 24-30 inches long and sharpened on one end. The wood was driven into a continuous vertical crack and secured by other wooden strips that ran parallel to the crack. On July 4, 1893, people came from over 100 miles away to witness the first formal ascent of Devils Tower. Two years later Rogers' wife duplicated the feat on another July 4th and became the first woman to reach the summit.

INYAN KARA

Another sky pillar is Inyan Kara, the mountain within a mountain. In order to get to the mountain, one has to cross pastureland and navigate a rutted, rocky road way back to a deserted set of log buildings.

Shadows on the buildings were short and accented the logs' vertical stacking. Behind the weathered wood, slopes of ponderosa pine rose skyward; to the west, horses grazed. Lame Deer said,

For bringing us the horse we could almost forgive you for bringing us whiskey. Horses make a landscape look more beautiful.

Their manes fluttered as the wind blew the sea of grass, and the prairie cone flowers danced with lupine and capers. Blue flax reflected the sky and shimmered like small suspended pools of water. There were butterflies on the bergamot and clovers, and mountain bluebirds flew in and out of the cabin holes.

As we moved up the steep slopes toward Inyan Kara, sometimes grabbing trees for hand help, our bodies leaned forward and made a difficult angle for our legs to step up. We drew deep gasping breaths, and it felt good.

We moved to a flat spot, and the vegetation was less dense. Here red-breasted nuthatches yelled "ink, ink" in their own peculiar nasal twang, and an Audubon's warbler sat in the dark foliage and sang and glowed. Brown creepers worked industriously up the tree trunks toward the descending nuthatches, and juncoes bounced on the forest floor among the holly and harebells.

The slope ended on a circular ridge. We walked between the pines and watched swifts dart across the sky and disappear over the rim. The rock changed from sedimentary to volcanic, and we climbed a mound of igneous rubble to what we expected to be the peak. Then the name Inyan Kara became reality, for before us spread a deep, curving valley outlined in a donut of sandstone and limestone. From its midst a monolith of rock soared upward.

We walked to its base and touched the rock. It was as if we were touching some sacred symbol of inner strength that the Earth had thrust upward from its molten soul. We moved up the rock to its airy peak where stonecrop, harebells, gumweed, and prickly pear basked in the sunlight. Wind-shaped ponderosa was here, along with junipers, but the top was mostly rock and patches of June grass and woodsia fern, along with short stalked flowers of white, purple, and yellow. On top, there was a broken jar filled with notes from others who had been here. There was also one name carved in the rock — Custer '74. George Armstrong Custer, the symbol of white invasion into the Black Hills, had stopped here and climbed to this summit.

On July 23, 1874, Custer brought his scientific team and two company of cavalry to the base of Inyan Kara. His campsite and the graves of two of his men are four miles east of the peak. He left the cavalry and went to the peak with Colonel Ludlow Donaldson and a few others. It was Donaldson who had carved Custer's name. I ran my fingers along the old chisel marks and touched a part of history.

There was the expedition of Lieutenant Warren who traveled north from Fort Laramie in 1857. He was the topographic engineer for Colonel "White Whiskers" Harney, who was in Utah for the Mormon Wars at the time. His assignment was to learn what lay behind the treaty boundaries, to satisfy the terrible curiosity of his nation.

In the land beneath this mountain, Warren met Miniconjou Sioux herding bison. Indian guards informed Warren that he must not move into the grazing ground, for white men were destroyers and their very smell ruined buffalo hunting grounds.

A council resulted with Warren and Chief Four Horns and his nephew Sitting Bull. The essence of that conference was a statement that the Black Hills had been there longer than both Indian and white and they were considered hallowed ground. The cavalry party was in violation of the treaty. The chiefs agreed that further travel would not be allowed; Lieutenant Warren accepted and withdrew.

The year after Custer's party, gold lured another government party, the Jenny-Newton Survey, to invade Indian territory. Dr. V. T. McGillycuddy, the chief topographer, climbed the peak where he found the Custer carving. His view of the mountains was obliterated by smoke because the Indians were burning the grasslands.

The year after Custer, still another group visited Inyan Kara. Joe Reynolds and his party bribed government men at Fort Laramie to ferry them across the Platte River. From there the trespassers moved north, climbing each large promontory to look for French Creek. They worked their way in an arc east through Spearfish and south to French Creek. They sought the gold of Custer's expedition.

Inyan Kara is a miniature Black Hills, volcanic rock pushed up by a violent earth through layers of ocean sediment. The sediment is tilted, and the soft layers are eroded. It is also part of the plumbing system of a volcano that never happened, something geologists call a laccolith.

The maze of volcanic flow was complex and massive, ranging over the entire north end of the mountain range. But the flow never erupted. Instead it cooled in the pipes and would never have seen daylight if the covering earth had not eroded.

The monuments in this system are the Missouri Buttes, Devils Tower, Bear Lodge Mountains, Sundance Mountain, Green Mountain, Inyan Kara, Black Buttes, Nigger Hill, Mineral Hill, Crow Peak, Citadel Rock, Ragged Top Mountain, Custer Peak, and Bear Butte. However, the last of my sky pillars would not be from this group. Indeed, it would be the granddaddy of the Black Hills, the heart of the mountains — Harney Peak.

HARNEY PEAK

Harney Peak is the strongest symbol in my sky pillars, for it represents the coming together of many factors — geology, plants and animals. Red men sought sacred images and sustenance, while European descendants sought wealth and the fulfillment of their fantasies. Two cultures with legacies of the east and the west had crossed great barriers of time and space to meet and to test the ability of diverse ideologies to coexist. It was in the shadow of Harney Peak that cultures clashed and the nation of the Indian ceased. Harney Peak is the center of the Black Hills, the center of the world. We followed a high trail that put us next to the face of Little Devils Tower, and we moved to the granite spires across the valley. These were heady outcroppings around which cloud banks swirled. Beside us was Harney Peak. Black Elk had stood in the prairies to the east, and pointed toward that peak, and said,

There, when I was young, the spirits took me in my vision to the center of the earth and showed me all the good things in the sacred hoop of the world.

In his vision, Black Elk had council with the powers of the west, the north, the east, the south, the sky, and the Earth. At the end of his vision, Black Elk heard the sun singing. This sky pillar was the mountain in his dream. At Harney Peak all the directions met and the sky touched the earth.

I looked at the rock and thought of a conversation I had had with Paul Gries of the geology department of the Rapid City School of Mines. Harney Peak was indeed the center of the Black Hills. Seventy to 60 million years ago the granite dome beneath The Hills began to move. The flat ocean bottom rose as the shock waves of the Rocky Mountain formation sent tremors through the earth.

Like a mirror to the past, the Black Hills rose as a dome and stopped, the first step in the formation of many segments of the Rockies, frozen in time, as each range to the west reflected more and more pressures and deformation. The layers that covered the granite were raised like the layers around Inyan Kara, and years of climatic pressures wore down and washed away soft ridges, leaving concentric circles of rock surrounding The Hills.

A drive to the center is a trip through time. Sandstones and limestones give way to folded metamorphic rocks that glisten in the road cuts. These were sedimentary rocks too, but they were older and closer to the granite when it was still hot magma; the heat and pressure of the granite formation changed these rocks and reshaped their layering.

The Black Hills rose, and volcanic ash swept into the swamps and estuaries, burying the life that had been there, but the uplands did not keep building the area to the east. Eventually the waters that carved away the top of the Black Hills dome also carved through the soft grey sediments that earlier rivers had deposited, and the Badlands came into being.

Harney Peak is in the middle of the fossil and rock volume of earth history. In fact, the geographic center of the fifty states lies just north of The Hills on Two Top Peak. On a fairly round globe an argument can be made for any spot as the middle, but certainly Black Elk's claim for Harney Peak is an acceptable one.

Harney Peak's story does not stop with Black Elk. As with so many of the sky pillars, General Custer's name must also be put into the story. Custer traversed a place he named Floral Valley. There the hardened troopers were so overwhelmed with the beauty of the flowers that they decorated the mules' harnesses and slipped petals into their notebooks for their wives. The band played on, and the party was in grand spirits when a crane flew off a ledge, glided down the valley, and was shot by Custer.

It was in this mood that Custer's troops reached the valley of the French Creek, south of the Harney Peak area. Here the enlisted men played baseball, and the miners panned for gold until a strike was made. Then everyone's thoughts turned to the yellow metal.

Custer and an escort commanded by Lieutenant Varnum celebrated with a ride through the heavily timbered ravines to Harney Peak. Custer and Ludlow made the ascent. At the top they named two prominent peaks in the north for General Terry and General Custer. Ludlow described the return trip as being a struggle against almost every possible obstacle — rocks, creeks, marshes, willow and aspen thickets, pine timber, dead and fallen trees, steep hillsides, and precipitous ravines. They reached camp by following Lieutenant Varnum's signal fires.

It was a day of many glories. The first Black Hills baseball game ended with a score of Actives-11, Athletes-6; a champagne dinner was held for some officers; the glee club serenaded the group; and shovels, picks, tentpins, bowie knives, pans, plates, and tin cups were being used to mine for gold. Even Sarah Campbell, the black cook who was the first non-Indian woman in the Black Hills, got caught up in the prospecting fever.

On August 2, 1874, Custer wrote a letter to his wife which included the following paragraph:

I did not hope to have my wagon-train with me, and here it has followed me everywhere. We have discovered a rich and beautiful country. We have had no Indian fights and will have none. We have discovered gold without a doubt, and probably other valuable metals. All are well, and have been the entire trip.

As I walked back from the Peak, the snow was falling in large flakes. Gargantuan granite rocks seemed to grow as we approached them. Our hike took us through a beaver meadow that was filled with the tracks and signs of mule deer. For a while we sat beneath a rock ledge and watched the land turn white. Then we made our way back to Sylvan Lake and left the center of the earth.

CHAPTER 6 # FORT ROBINSON

In my journal I wrote, "This is silly. Here we sit in the Granada with Mendelssohn playing on the cassette player, and a rainstorm outside. We are in Fort Robinson State Park in Nebraska, parked outside a stable in a driving rain and hoping no one finds us before morning."

I wanted to see the southern grasslands, the only approach to the Black Hills that I had never taken. This was the route of the Sidney Stage, north of Scotts Bluff and the Oregon Trail. The land was rolling and green; the Medicine Bow Mountains stood in the west, catching the setting sun.

Fort Robinson is in the midst of high cliffs and forests near the White River (the carver of the Bad Lands). It is north of the Nebraska Sand Hills and Agate Fossil Mounds National Monument, where important mammal fossils were discovered.

It was as unlikely a place for the after-effects of the Little Big Horn as Fort Meade on the other side of the Black Hills, but the closing chapter for the Indians began here.

The most recognized warriors of the Sioux nation were Crazy Horse — the cavalry man, the heart of the Indians — and Sitting Bull — a visionary, the soul of the Sioux. Together they were the heart and soul of the Sioux nation's resistance.

When Crazy Horse was twelve and called Curly, he had a vision in which a man came riding light and airy on a spotted war horse. Arrows and lead balls went toward the dream figure but did not hurt him. The man rode through a violent storm and came out with a zigzag of lightning painted on his cheek and hailstone marks on his body. Over his head flew a red-backed hawk. The man's own people came running to him with arms out and making a great noise. In the man's mind were anguish and pride.

When Curly told his father the dream a few years later, his father knew that it was his son in the vision and he gave him his own name, Crazy Horse.

Crazy Horse fought in Red Cloud's War and was a major force in the Fetterman Massacre and the Wagon Box Fight at Fort Kearney. He fought and won and refused to be put on a reservation. After the Treaty of 1868 he moved north and joined forces with the Cheyenne and with his chief, Sitting Bull.

Sitting Bull had been involved in the retaliatory actions that followed the Minnesota Uprising of 1862; he had fought General Sully at Killdeer Mountain in North Dakota. From Little Crow he had learned how the American government treated reservation Indians.

As a warrior he exhibited an ability to locate animals for the hunters. To a hunter society this was a crucial talent. In 1866 he was made chief of the northern tribes, with Crazy Horse as his subordinate chief.

Sitting Bull was willing to abide by the Treaty of 1868, but the rush for gold in the Black Hills destroyed the peace. The Arapaho, Cheyenne, and Sioux gathered at his camp in Montana where he headed the war council of the confederacy and defied the 1875 dictum that all Sioux return to their reservations by the end of January, 1876.

He became the spiritual leader of the confederacy on the Little Bighorn. Prior to the Custer battle he performed a Sun Dance that foretold an Indian victory. The dance wore him out so that he could not participate in the battle, but it was a powerful inspiration for his confederacy and the warriors. Crazy Horse, just eight days after his victory over Crook at the Rosebud River, was the victorious field general. Following the battle, Crazy Horse took 800 men back to Sioux territory for supplies, but he was pursued relentlessly by General Miles. After a devastating attack on his people at Wolf Mountain, Red Cloud urged Crazy Horse to give up. Four months later he did, and the army took him to Fort Robinson. The spring that Crazy Horse surrendered, Dull Knife and the Cheyennes surrendered to General McKenzie, and Sitting Bull took his warriors north to live in "Grandmother's Land" (Canada).

Crazy Horse's search for peace was not destined to be successful. The authorities heard rumors that he was planning to make trouble again and

ordered him locked in the guard house. He resisted and was bayoneted in the abdomen. Major Lemly recorded his last words:

I was not hostile to the white man, occasionally my young men would attack a party of the Crows or Arickarees, and take their ponies, but just as often, they were the assailants. We had buffalo for food, and their hides for clothing, and we preferred the chase to a life of idleness and the bickerings and jealousies, as well as the frequent periods of starvation at the Agencies.

But the Gray Fox (General Crook) came out in the snow and bitter cold, and destroyed my village. All of us would have perished of exposure and hunger had we not recaptured our ponies.

Then Long Hair (Custer) came in the same way. They say we massacred him, but he would have massacred us had we not defended ourselves and fought to the death. Our first impulse was to escape with our squaws and papooses, but we were so hemmed in that we had to fight. . . .

Again the Gray Fox sent soldiers to surround me and my village; but I was tired of fighting. All I wanted was to be let alone, so I anticipated their coming and marched all night to Spotted Tail Agency while the troops were approaching the site of my camp.

Touch-the-Clouds knows how I settled at Spotted Tail Agency, in peace. The agent told me I must first talk with the big white chief of the Black Hills. Under his care I came here unarmed, but instead of talking, they tried to confine me, and when I made an effort to escape, a soldier ran his bayonet into me.

"I HAVE SPOKEN."

At the close of his speech, Crazy Horse, in a weak and tremulous voice, broke into the Sioux death song. Instantly, there were two answering calls from his parents who were not admitted to see their son.

The heart was gone, and only the soul remained, but he was in Canada. The death grip was on the entire Sioux nation.

In 1879 Fort Robinson was part of the next step in Indian annihilation. Dull Knife and Little Wolf, along with 300 followers, two-thirds of them women and children, left the reservation in Oklahoma. The people of the prairie and mountains could not adjust to the dusty south. They were homesick and came to the Black Hills to live out their lives in peace. In Nebraska each chief took half of the homeless refugees and parted company.

Dull Knife and his band moved across the Sand Hills and were cut down by a blizzard. The 3rd Cavalry found the starving Indians and lobbed shells into their ranks until they surrendered. They were taken to some unused barracks where they were locked up and fed until January 5, when Captain Wessells decided to starve them until they agreed to return to Oklahoma.

In desperation the Cheyenne broke free of the

barracks. During the melee that followed 50 Cheyenne, mostly women and children, were shot or bludgeoned. A month later Dull Knife and a few survivors arrived at the Pine Ridge Reservation and surrendered. The authorities finally decided that it was all right for them to stay.

Two years later Sitting Bull returned from Canada and gave himself up to authorities at Fort Buford under a promise of amnesty.

I surrender this rifle to you through my son. I wish him to learn the habits of whites. I wish it to be remembered that I was the last man of my tribe to surrender my rifle, and this day have given it to you. Whatever you have to give, or whatever you have to say, I would like to receive of here now, for I don't wish to be kept in darkness longer. I have sent several messengers here from time to time, but none of them have returned with news. The other chiefs, Crow King and Gall, have not wanted me to come and I have never received good news from them. I now wish to be allowed to live this side of the line **(Canada)** or the other, as I see fit. I wish to continue my old life of hunting, but would like to be allowed to trade on both sides of the line. This is my country, and I don't wish to be compelled to give it up. My heart was very sad at having to leave the Great Mother's country. She has been a friend to me, but I want my children to grow up in our native country. . . .I wish to have all my people live together upon one reservation of our own on the Little Missouri. I left several families at Wood Mountain, and between there and Qu'Appelle. I have many people among the Yanktons at Poplar Creek, and I wish all of them and those who have gone to Standing Rock to be collected together upon my reservation.

After his return, Sitting Bull was imprisoned in Fort Randall for two years. Dull Knife died at the Pine Ridge Reservation toward the end of Sitting Bull's imprisonment.

In 1884 Sitting Bull was released into the custody of the Standing Rock Reservation and was allowed to parade around the world as a curiosity in Buffalo Bill's Wild West Show. The soul of the Indian was being treated like a cigar store statue.

If the Indians were to gain their status on the plains again, they needed more than good land, bison, and horses. They needed their spirit rekindled.

In this depressed state, Wovoka, a Paiute, offered the Indians a hope, a dream. He talked of a Messiah who would drive the white man from the land and restore the Indian to power. He told of Ghost Shirts that would stop the rifle's bullet. It was everything a fallen people wanted to hear. The Ghost Dance became a chance to hold on, a possibility that they might regain their dignity.

The whites became fearful. Was it an uprising? When would the shooting start?

At Wounded Knee there was frustration in 1890 and again in 1973. The creek was dry, the land was frozen, and there was a chill in the air that went beyond temperature.

Big Foot's band had danced the Ghost Dance here, but the Messiah did not come. Instead, guns went off; and men, women, children, and an aged chief died in the snow.

The Ghost Dance was the prairie Indians' last gasp, and even though Sitting Bull was not active in it, the military decided that he was too strong a leader to be free during this time. He was arrested and fatally shot by two Indian policemen. The soul of the Indian nation was gone.

Prairie grasses

Purple Cone flower

Badlands

INDIAN
IMAGES

Sioux mother and child

Yellow Cone flower

Bison in Badlands

INDIAN
IMAGES

Yucca flowers

Prickly Pear Cactus

Sheeptable Mountain

Sheeptable Mountain

Badlands — rich prairie grasses of valley floor

INDIAN
Images

Badlands

Moon setting on Badlands

Prairie homestead

Winter in Badlands

Climbing the tower

Prairie dog

Rappelling down tower

INDIAN
Images

PART II —

THE LURE OF THE MOUNTAINS

CHAPTER 7 THE BLACK MOUNTAINS

The Black Hills are mountains of rock, yet they are called hills. Their height would be great in the mountains far to the east, but they get dwarfed by their mountain neighbors to the west. They are a mirage on the prairie. No one expects them in the grasslands of South Dakota.

The mountain men are associated with the high Rockies, but there is a place for them in the Black Hills lore too. These were hard men, overland voyageurs who sought beaver pelts and other furs. The Verendrye brothers were the first trapper-traders to explore this region. Their father had been the chief of a post on Lake Nipigon, where Cree Indians brought news of a great river that flowed west into a "great still water that tasted bad." By 1742 Verendrye was racked with illness, but his sons were young, healthy, and anxious. Their journal records the following:

On January 1st, 1743, we were in sight of the mountains. The number of the warriors exceeded two thousand; with their families they made a considerable band, advancing all the way through a magnificent prairie where animals are plentiful. At night there was singing and shouting, and they wept continually, begging us to accompany them to war. I resisted steadily, saying that we were sent to pacify the land and not to stir it up.

The Verendryes were disappointed in not getting into the mountains. A war was raging among the Indians, and they were not permitted to go to the highlands. They had come across the Missouri River in North Dakota, crossed the Heart, Cannonball, Grand, Moreau, and Big Cheyenne Rivers, and reached the area around Bear Butte. They then followed the Bad River to the Missouri where they buried a lead plate near what would become Pierre, South Dakota. From here they moved north again with the first explorer's vision of the mountains.

For the next few decades the trader-explorers never came close to the mountains. Names like Dorion, D'Eglise, Garreau, and Loisel recall the Frenchmen who made friends with Sioux, Mandan, and Arikara, married their women and lived in the Indian villages. By the War of 1812 these tribes were ready to back French interests, but the enigmatic Manuel Lisa managed to calm the Indian threats.

The Frenchmen stayed on the Bad, White, Cheyenne, and Moreau Rivers rather than going to the mountains because the bison was the main fur here, not the beaver. Their robes and blankets would be sent to those who trapped in the lake country, and pemmican would be shipped for pack food.

The United States had only one major expedition to the area during this time, that of Lewis and Clark in 1804. The Corps of Discovery included the first black man to the area, Clark's slave York, who was a subject of great Indian curiosity. There were many encounters with local tribes, but none of them led the Corps to The Hills.

The Missouri River remained dominant because of its travel potential. In 1807 the first battle between white travelers and western Indians took place on the Missouri, and it was along this river that Crooks, McLellan, Lisa, Hunt, and Astor added their names to the region's rich history. Trading was on the upsweep and was definitely leaning toward the mountains.

In 1823 a second major clash between Indians and whites took place on the Missouri. The Arikara attacked the Ashley party of fur traders and wounded or killed one quarter of the contingent. This led to retribution by Colonel Leavenworth and mountain man Joshua Pilcher. Emotions were high, and the rush was on.

Trader Major Henry was intent on opening the west. He sent one group of explorers to the north of The Hills and a second group to cross them. In this manner the greatest adventure of the mountain men began.

The northern group included many mountain men who were already well known, like old Hugh Glass, as well as neophytes like Jim Bridger and John Fitzgerald. They were seasoned enough to react to dangers and young enough to call on strength and resiliency where experience was lacking.

There were rules to prevent the mountain men from getting separated from the group or getting killed. Every man was to keep his gun within reach at all times, but Hugh found raspberries too much of a temptation to resist. It was too late to grab a gun when he found a she-bear grizzly and cub in the same berry patch with him. The result was a clubbing such as Hugh had never known.

Major Henry was in a quandary. Glass was mauled,

unconscious, and sure to die, but he couldn't be moved in his present condition and a mountain man never deserts his partner. The decision was to have Bridger and Fitzgerald watch him die and then bury him. For doing this they would each receive an extra half year's salary.

The rookies were in a tight spot. Sioux and Arikara were in the area, another bear might come in, or the rest of the group might encounter other problems. Hugh was unconscious, but he wouldn't die.

Finally, Fitz convinced Jim that they had to go. It was late in the year, the Indians would find them, and Hugh was going to die anyway. They were northeast of The Hills on the Grand River and a long way from Henry's post. They decided to leave and tell the others that Glass had died. Their plan had one flaw, however; Glass refused to die. Armed only with a razor, he crawled and scrambled two hundred miles to a fort.

The second party under Major Henry was led by Jedediah Smith and included William Sublette, Ed Rose, Tom Fitzpatrick, and James Clyman. They were to strike a straight route to the Black Hills, cross the mountains and the Powder and Tongue Rivers, and go to the Big Horns. They were to be the first white travelers in the Black Hills.

They left Fort Kiowa and traveled across dry, rolling, desolate highlands into the valley of White Clay Creek which Clyman described as "running thick with a white sediment and resembling cream in appearance, but of a sweetish, pugent (sic) taste."

Despite the warning of the guide against using the water too freely because of its "excessive costiveness," they gulped it down and suffered nausea on their 24 hour march to the next water supply. They described their next campsite as being so full of prickly pear that there was no place to spread a blanket.

Their guide deserted them, and the party spread out to look for water. Clyman wrote, "We ware not only long but wide and it appeared like we might never all collect together again." Clyman found water, shot off his gun, and fell in. Each mountain man did the same.

When Jedediah Smith arrived, two men were still missing. In the heat they had passed out, and Smith had buried them in sand to preserve their body moisture. He took water back to them and found them still alive.

We packed up and crossed the White Clay River and proceeded north westernly over a dry roling country for several days meeting with a Buffaloe now and then which furnished us with provision for at least one meal each day our luck was to fall in with the Ogela tiribe of Sioux whare traded a few more horses and swaped of some of our more ordinay.

After crossing the Cheyenne River they rode into the southern Badlands and Clyman recorded the following:

A tract of country whare no vegetation of any kind existed beeing worn into knobs and gullies and extremely uneven a loose grayish coloured soil very soluble in water running thick as it could move of a pale whitish coular and remarkably adhesive there on a misty rain while we were in this pile of ashes and it loded down our horses feet in great lumps it looked a little remarkable that not a foot of level land could be found the narrow ravines going in all manner of directions and the cobble mounds of a regular taper from top to bottom all of them of the precise same angle and the tops sharp the whole of this region is moveing to the Misourie River as fast as rain and thawing of snow can carry it.

Their adventures continued into the Black Hills, which they expected to be the eastern source of the Powder River.

going dwn a small stream we came into a kenyon and pushed ourselves down so far that our horses had no room to turn while looking for a way out it became dark by unpacking and leading our animals down over slipery rocks three of us got down to a nice open glade whare we killed a Buffaloe and fared sumpiously that night while the rest of the company remained in the kenyon without room to lie down.

James Clyman's diary also described the change that transpired as they left the plains:

At length we arrived at foot of black hills which rises in verry slight elevation above the common plain we entered a pleasant undulating region cool and refreshing so different from the hot dusty planes we have been so long passing over and here we found hazlnuts and ripe plumbs a luxury not expected.

Like their contemporaries to the north, the Smith party suffered swift and unexpected grizzly attacks.

Grissly did not hesitate a moment but sprang on the cap[t] taking him by the head first pitching sprawling on the earth. . . .

none of us having any surgical knowledge what was to be done one said come take hold and he would say why not you. . . .

I asked the cap[t] what was the best he said one or 2 for water and if you have a needle and thread get it out. . . .

the bear had taken nearly all his head in his capcious mouth close to his left eye on one side and clos to his right ear on the other and laid the skull bare to near the crown of the head leaving a white streak whare his teeth passed. . . .

I told him I could do nothing for his Eare O you must try to stitch up some way or other said he. . . .

the captain was able to mount his horse and ride to camp where we pitched a tent the onley one we had and made him as comfortable as circumstances would permit this gave us a lisson on the character of the grissly baare which we did not forget.

Within ten days Jedediah Smith could ride out. For the rest of his life he carried a scar from the first successful crossing of the Black Hills.

CHAPTER 8 # THE CANYONS

The rains of The Hills have etched alluring pathways through the limestone ridges — innocent openings that wind through a labyrinth of cliffs, leading, like silent sirens, to the heart of the mountains themselves.

I explored many of these canyons by foot and by car. My roaming included the startling color experience of Red Canyon where uranium exploration threatens the beauty of the land. I drove through Boulder Canyon where rock walls seemed to bulge out over the creek and the waters tumbled through tortuous slalom courses in the rocks. I drove through the Grand Canyon of Sand and Cold Springs Creeks between Beulah and Hardy, and I explored the most famous of the Black Hills Canyons, Spearfish, and its unknown partner to the west, Fish Hatchery Gulch.

I wandered in and out of the valley floors — driving roads, climbing high places, and probing into side streams. In the depths of the canyons I felt as though I were in the bowels of the mountains.

My first canyon experience was in Spearfish. It was one of THE places to go. I was anxious that everything be a positive experience, but I was escorted into the Canyon by miles of powerlines and poorly zoned buildings. I feared that the Canyon would be one large disillusionment. Then I passed the National Forest boundary; there were fewer wires and fewer buildings, and the Canyon was even more beautiful than I had expected.

The creek was rushing between two white shores and plunging into a dark chasm of almost black spruce. The water seemed darker and bluer because everything else was without color, and it danced and frothed in a rocky bed. A little grey figure perched tentatively on a rock, walked down the rock's icy side, slipped its head into the water, and drifted to the next rock. The dipper got out, dipped, bowed, and hurried to another pool. In an erratic bobbing and zigzagging manner it moved upstream and out of sight. The little grey bird was too busy surviving to look at the snowfall or the bearded birdwatcher.

In other seasons the stream is alive too. On a hot July afternoon I watched families sitting on the rocks with their feet and their children in the water. I also remember a group of hot and leg-weary bicyclers doing a quick skinny dip in the stream. The creek is a source of drinking water for Spearfish so people are prohibited from wading or swimming in it, but on a hot summer day that is about as easy to control as prohibiting breathing.

I pursued a black headed grosbeak in the oak and pine stands of the canyon, but had no success. The combination of oak and pine is an unusual occurrence, and a favorite of this large-billed yellow bird. I also pursued the beauty of the floral gardens. Nowhere did I find greater rainbows of color than in the meadows above Roughlock Falls. Yellows were captured by goldenrod, primrose, and the delicate segolily (mariposa); daisy and anemones added white; blue was captured by penstemon and lobellia; and pinks and purples were added by verbena, joe-pye-weed, fireweed, and big topped wild bergamot.

Fish played in the cold pools below Timber Gulch. They sat in the shade of floating leaves and darted between shadows. They seemed as natural as the dipper, but the little trout were not native to The Hills. Game fish are not native to the state, so back in 1891 the Federal Government started planting brook trout in Spearfish Creek and the streams near Rapid City. The native fish were minnows, chubs, and suckers — including the hard headed sucker found in no other part of the world.

A small native sideswimmer, gammerous, was such a prolific animal that while fish were being shipped into The Hills, this little crustacean was being shipped out to be established as fish food in other states.

In 1899 fish hatcheries at Yellowstone and Spearfish were established which would serve as partners in the next few decades. Fishery's men made trips to Yellowstone to get fish eggs and transported them to Spearfish on horse-drawn wagons. The eggs were packed in ice to maintain the proper temperatures, and melt water provided a fresh water source. It was an ambitious project and also a very successful one until mine dumps began to poison many of the streams.

In Sand Creek Canyon I wanted to see the vistas, the wide sweep of rock as it caressed the valley floor and guided the sunbeams down from the sky, but each time I stepped back to look at the whole, I found my attention focused on a part. I looked at a curving wall of rock that bulged at the top, but soon I was caught up in the wheeling, circular flight of the violet-green swallow and the startling rocketry of the white-throated swifts.

A rock cliff rose above the treetops of the valley and was decorated with pine trees across its surface. I looked at the shading and soon was following the echoes of a familiar scream. Two red-tailed hawks were taking turns swaying in a pine tree and soaring out over the cliff's edge.

A kestrel yelled "ki-ki-ki" from a roost in a cliff side, and a turkey vulture came over the eastern edge. Its wings were set back in a wide "V" shape, and the primaries seemed to be made of sunbeams.

Chipping sparrows gathered gravel from the roadbed, and a streak of yellow moved quickly from pines to cottonwoods and sang a fluid tanager song in the leaves. The western tanagers were beginning to symbolize the Black Hills for me. Their yellow, black, red, and white colors were excitement and variety.

They represented the colors of the races of mankind that have settled in this land. The white and black miners and soldiers, the largest Chinatown outside of San Francisco and New York, and the constant presence of the Indians were all part of this colorful singer.

CHAPTER 9 GOLD

In Whitewood Canyon I waded into a stream that only a short time ago had been silver with arsenic from mine operations and was thick with the effluent of a city sewage disposal. Fortunately, that has ceased, and I felt safe probing the stream sediments with my gold pan. I wanted to find out what it had been like for Ezra Kind when he snuck into The Hills to look for illegal gold. How did it feel when Horatio Ross found gold with Custer's expedition in 1874?

I did not expect to know the sensation that Potato Creek Johnny experienced. At four feet three inches tall, Johnny must have been the smallest of the gold seekers in The Hills. His real name was John Perrault; but after finding a 7 3/4 ounce nugget in Potato Creek, his last name was seldom heard. I could understand his friendship with birds and chipmunks and porcupines, for I have been talking with animals for years. It was easy to realize why he would feel so comfortable with children since they were the only ones he could look in the eyes. I can even understand his winter pleasure in the violin and guitar. But I will never know what it is like to hold a fortune in my hand.

That would be like understanding how the Manuel brothers must have felt years after selling the Homestake Mine when they saw the riches that it brought to the Hearst family. They weren't swindled; they had intended to sell any strike they made since they didn't have the capital to develop it.

Mose and Fred Manuel grew up in Minnesota, one of the most goldless states around. Mose prospected in Montana, Utah, Nevada, California, and Alaska in search of illusive fortune. In 1874 he returned from Alaska to Portland where he intended to take passage to Africa to look for his fortune. While he waited for passage across the ocean, he bought a newspaper and read about gold discoveries in the Black Hills. This one newspaper story changed his destiny. His brother Fred met him in Helena, and the two of them prospected around Custer for a while without success. They moved north with Hank Harney and detected quartz in Gold Run Creek in 1876. Where they found the white rock, they expected to find yellow ore. They sold their claim to George Hearst and his California associates.

Hearst had been a worker in the St. Louis lead mines before moving to California with the 49ers. In that strike he had amassed $15 million. The Manuels found and sold the Old Abe Mine, and afterward Harney went back to Iowa while the Manuels returned to Minnesota, satisfied with their success.

In 1877 Hearst shipped an eight stamp mill by rail from San Francisco to Sidney, Nebraska, and from there by oxcart to Lead, South Dakota. The Homestake Mine was destined to be the richest gold mine in the United States and the only one to re-open after World War II.

The Manuels and Potato Creek Johnny did not work in seclusion. Each stake was small and surrounded by other diggings. Everybody wanted to strike a quartz vein, but they were also working placer claims in the stream beds as well as the gravel of ancient stream beds high on the canyon walls. A contemporary legend says that the Black Hills are a mound over the grave of Paul Bunyan's blue ox. Perhaps it would be better to call it a gold miner's ant mound, with each creek another tunnel.

The picks and shovels must have echoed through The Hills like thunder; each find was relayed from claim to claim, up and down the valleys, quicker than a telegram. People outside The Hills heard the good news and chose to ignore the failures, so The Hills kept getting more and more crowded.

Gold is a very heavy metal, and this causes it to sink when other things float away and to fall when other things blow away. That was the simple principle of placer mining. A placer miner dug no shafts and drilled no holes — he shoveled. He shoveled through centuries of gravel to get down to bedrock where, if he was lucky, the heavy bits of gold would be found.

I knew the rules of panning: bring a pan, shovel and pick, magnifying glass, and magnet. I had a pan. Slow-moving streams are better than fast ones, but I was taking whatever was available, so I searched the sediment in an eddy behind a big flat piece of rock.

The recommended procedure is to fill the pan level with gravel, set it in six inches of water, and knead it. Then throw out the heavy rocks and pebbles, shake the pan vigorously, and, with the pan tilted, slosh the water around so that the light materials are washed away. A magnet can then be used to remove some of the non-gold metals.

I didn't have a magnet so I ran my hand through the collection of stones, and my eyes caught the glitter of color. Pyrite, fool's gold, in square brassy crystals was common as were other bits of color I couldn't be sure of. I played with the pan for a time, but I soon got bored. I thought of the sluice boxes and rockers all up and down Whitewood Creek, Whitetail Creek, Yellow Creek, and every other waterway lined with broken men and dreams. It was fun, but gold is just another yellow rock. Only a government can make it worth a life or a loaf of bread.

I went looking for a ghost town.

CHAPTER 10 WINDOWS WITHOUT GLASS

In the 1800's the towns of The Hills were far greater in number than they are today. There was a time when Tinton was an energetic town serving the successful black miners of Nigger Hill as well as the hopefuls of many other claims. There was Tigerville with a population of 200, a post office, two stores, and the King Solomon Mine. Cascade Springs sat on a stream that never froze; it had a bank, a bowling alley, a club, two stores, one hotel, and 25 people who dreamed of a railroad line that never came.

In 1878 Richford had 500 people, 200 houses, a solid block of stores with wooden canopied sidewalks, and the Evangeline, Minnesota, Stand-by and Balkan Mines. By 1900 there were 48 inhabitants. Now a garter snake lies by a puddle and gorges itself on tadpoles while the waters evaporate, leaving the legless amphibians landlocked. That is the only sign of life on a hot summer afternoon.

Where are the dreams of Three Forks, Tin Reef, and Spokane? Who mines the Cleopatra, the Wasp, the Etta, and the Holy Terror now? These are ghost towns where the winds move through windows without glass. Everywhere there are stories waiting to be told of ordinary people caught in the hysteria of quick wealth, sudden moves, and tragic events.

The stores were built with false front architecture, the rage of the entire west. These made a single story look like two, and a two-story appear to have three. It was the American myth. Everyone wanted to be bigger and more important than they really were. It was a worthless deceit, but few people wanted to be different; and the false front could always be used as a billboard. Steps to the second story were outside because it was easier and cheaper to build that way, and it saved space inside the building.

Doctors were sought by every town of reasonable size. Cholera, typhoid, diphtheria, pneumonia, pleurisy, smallpox, measles, and influenza ravaged small towns. Even though the doctor might be poorly trained and ill equipped, he still offered hope, one of the most difficult of all commodities to obtain. In 1880, 224 people died of diphtheria in sparsely settled South Dakota.

Water supplies were often destroyed by the mines that supported the town. Decay, food poisoning, and industrial accidents added to the community woes, and the doctor the people turned to was often one who came west because he had failed in the east. Treatment was so bad that the Dakota territories passed a law making it a misdemeanor for an intoxicated doctor to poison a patient. If the victim died, the charge was changed to manslaughter.

Indian remedies gleaned from the woods offered the simplest and safest medicines, but the stores did not promote those things. No patent could be taken on a free-growing plant, and that meant no income. Advertisements promoted patent medicines, and the apothecary or the general store was the place to get "Pratt's Healing Ointment for Man and Beast." Peddlers sold "Grove's Tasteless Chill Tonic" which "makes children and adults as fat as pigs." Most medicines were little more than alcohol and a few pungent herbs. Even the most puritan household could take a little "medicine" before bed. "Hotsetter's Stomach Bitters" contained 44% alcohol, made its manufacturer a millionaire, and claimed to ward off:

Dyspepsia's pangs that rack and grind
The body and depress the mind;
Colics and dysenteric pains,
'Neath which the strong man's vigor wanes;
Bilious complaints, — those tedious ills,
Ne'er conquered yet by drastic pills;
Nervous prostration, mental gloom,
Heralds of madness or the tomb.

Dr. Ayer sold sarsaparilla, and Dr. Buckland had "Scotch Oats Essence" which "will positively cure sleeplessness, paralysis, opium habit, drunkenness, hysteria, neuralgia, sick headache, sciatica, ..." The public was gullible. Isolated on the prairies, they were even helpless. They took castoria and "PE-RU-NA" and unwittingly gave their children morphine with each spoonful of "Mrs. Winslow's Soothing Syrup."

Corresponding with the rise of the Black Hills boom was another manufacturing boom — packaged cereals. The lucky wife whose husband was bringing in gold dust could buy that precooked wheat cereal that Dr. John Kellogg had developed for his patients in Battle Creek, Michigan. Or they could buy his brother Tom's corn flakes. The cereal rush was on. Dr. Jackson in New York invented granola; Henry Perky in Denver worked out a method of shredding wheat; and Charles Post made an imitation granola — Grape Nuts.

The woods provided the fresh fruit and meat for most diets, but the store was the source of dry goods and candy and the foods that the family didn't get from their garden. The stores had posters to help you pick out your needs.

No town could run without transportation, and that meant horses, so the blacksmith shop was an open-air necessity. These were the early filling stations where a man could be respectable if his clothes and hands were dirty. This was a place to talk horses and other men's talk.

I leaned on the windowsill of a weathered building and watched the dust dance as a swirl of wind moved through the hollow rooms. This house had once been the center of a family's life and my thoughts traveled to an earlier time when a married man would return to his home after a day in the mines. He would join his family for supper that had been prepared over the wood burning stove. Then, they would sit by the fireplace. Perhaps the children would ask for a story about the covered wagon trip from Des Moines. The parents would look at each other and sigh; the mother would pat the father's hand, and he would relate:

You was just a young one then, couldn't speak or understand a word I said, kinda like the Injuns we met along the trail.

We signed up with Mr. Henry's wagon train after your mother and I decided it was time to either make our fortune or accept what we had. It was a tough decision, but we made it.

We traveled as a train, a parade of white-sheeted covered wagons pulled by a fine set of oxen. We sold everything we had to get it. There were no railroads that came here then. It was Injun country then, and Washington couldn't let the tracks go down until they owned the land.

Inside the wagon we piled everything we would need here. I took my tools and my fiddle, your mother took that old clock her granddad made, kitchen tools, a mirror — I still can't figure what she needed that for — her chest of linens, and a rocking chair.

She even slipped a couple of toys in there for you. Well, we also brought our stove and some flour and some seeds, and I brought my gun. Them days you had to be on the lookout for ambush and a gun was mighty handy to have. It also got us lots of suppers.

The sentinels would roust us about 4 A.M. The wagons would spill out sleepy-eyed people and their mutts. We'd take care of the horses and oxen while the ladies would cook up some good vittles for breakfast.

At 7 the whips cracked and the oxen moved against their yokes and the schooner would lurch forward. I would walk alongside the wagon while your mother nursed you on the wagon seat.

At sunset the wagons circled into rest position. The oxen were unyoked, and the wagons were attached to each other for protection. Your mother and the other ladies collected buffalo chips for the fire and boiled a pot of coffee to wash down the dust we ate all day. Some days I figured I'd eaten so much dust that I wouldn't have room for food in my stomach, but somehow the coffee always settled the mudball and let me get some of Ma's good cooking inside of me.

If it wasn't my turn to be on guard duty, I would play my fiddle, and we would dance and sing while the coyotes screamed in the distance.

Mother would look into the flickering fire and add,

There were tough times when I cried myself to sleep at night and wished I'd never left Iowa. The lonely graves we passed were a constant reminder of the danger we were in.

Then there were the storms. I remember one night when the lightning seemed to cut the sky in half, and the thunder grabbed the wagon and shook it. I knowed it was the thunder because the wind was blowing the wagon all night. It would sneak in the doorflap and billow the wagon cover with a terrible noise, but it weren't nothing like that thunderclap.

I was nearly ready to break into tears as I cradled your little head, but I looked out just then and saw the fellers scrambling in the rain, trying to hold down the canvas after it blowed down, but they couldn't do it. The tent was like a wild buffalo that night, and my tears turned to laughter.

Mainly I remember how small we were in fields without fences that stretched to the horizons. As the sun rose, its light seemed to rise from the roots of the grass, and the stalks would glow and the flowers would shine. It was beautiful, but I'll tell you I laughed and cried and hugged the first pine tree we came to.

Then the home would fill with fiddle music and settle into the night.

A well beside the ghostly home is hidden in the grass now; the bucket no longer plunges into the water. It seemed forlorn; but as I walked past, I felt the rut that had been worn by thousands of footsteps to the well. I could hear the grunts and groans as the son struggled beneath the water's weight, trying to be as strong as his father and trying not to show his effort.

Behind the house another building rested on its side. There was no floor, just three holes in a rough-hewn board staring into the middle of the old town site. All it needed was a well-thumbed catalog with pictures of "Whitman's Celebrated Hay, Straw and Wool Presses" and "Dr. Warner's Camel Hair Health Underwear."

The ghost towns sit in pine meadows, on dusty roads, and along old railroad grades. They sit silently, gracefully deteriorating, with empty post office boxes and rotting wooden sidewalks. Some stories are subtle, while others, like Irish Gulch Dance Hall, seem to shout with silence.

Bridal Veil Falls

Fishing Spearfish Creek

Spearfish Canyon area

Spearfish Canyon

Spearfish Canyon below Roughlock Falls

Edward Nielsen's goldmining cabin

Standby Stamp Mill — Rochford

PART III —

THE WILD WEST

CHAPTER 11 # THE BLACK HILLER

There is a degree of independence in the settlers of this land that must be admired, regardless of how ethical the taking of the Black Hills might have been. These people were individuals and they carved their own legends and folk tales in the land.

I was driving the road from Hulette to Alva when I spotted a farmer driving his horse-drawn hay wagon. Behind him was a cottonwood stream and the beginning of the Bear Lodge Mountains. The scene was too dramatic to pass up. I asked to take his picture, but he was more anxious to talk. I leaned on a fence post and tried to see the land through his eyes.

He stood tall on the wooden wagon, reins in one hand, and both arms leaning on the front rack. He wore a blue denim coat over blue and white coveralls. Both horses were reddish brown. One had white stockings, a white blaze down its face, and a white tail. The other had its entire left rear quarter covered with white like a saddle blanket that had slipped and was falling off. The surrounding ground was patchy brown and white, and the sides of the Bear Lodge Mountains were deep green-black.

His sentences were punctuated with "whoa" and "goddam it." He told me about Alva, a country town without logging or commerce which never was big, and had a dug-out store until the bridge was destroyed.

"It just took care of the farmers. Lots of towns used to be like that. If there were a few farmers in a region, someone had to give them supplies. People didn't jump on freeways and drive fifty miles to shopping centers in those days."

His in-laws had the first sawmill in the region. "It warn't a big one."

As he talked, his mind reached back into memories that he had not recently stirred. Even if they weren't in sequence, they still brought him pleasure. His eyes twinkled, and he leaned forward.

"Do you know how the road twists down the mountain ahead?

"I remember this old pistol. Well, he warn't really old then. He came down into Alva to buy a bottle of whiskey, and then he falls asleep on the way home,

and d'ya know them horses took him down all the mountian switchbacks and he doan even know it?"

He chuckled and tugged at the reins. "Whoa! Damn it!" The horses, impatient to move, stopped, then stutter-stepped forward. They leaned against their single trees and the wagon lurched. "Whoa, I said!" The reins jerked, and he leaned back towards me.

"I had a stallion got stubborn, reared back, and went right over me one time. He took off with my plow still attached and went right down this here road. Put a furrow right down the middle of it. He was an easy one to track.

"Only three of us use horses now. Don't know what they're going to do with this gas shortage.

"Just bought a new pair of boots," he announced. Then he walked to the edge of the wagon and showed them to me. They were black rubber and had eight buckles. I admired them and said that they were nice boots.

"Goddam things cost me $13!" He paused. "Hell, they had this thin dress rubber. What the hell good they going to do for a fella like me that's outside all the time? Most were made in Korea. I asked them why the hell they didn't get good American boots."

"Too much money?", I ventured.

"Ya. Why'n hell didn't them fellers in Washington put on a ceiling when they saw this happening back in the fifties?"

We talked of snows and winds, rains and melts. We looked at where the roads had been and where they were now.

"Things was a hell of a lot different around the turn of a century. We had people trying to homestead every 160 acres, and there was roads all over hell."

"I like horses. They seem to give a better feeling for the land than tractors do," I commented.

"Damn right they do!"

He talked with gestures from his mittened hands. His face was framed with an earflapped woolen hat, and his sparsely toothed mouth worked behind his weathered beard. He stroked his whiskers with the back of a mitten, and his wind-reddened cheeks beamed.

"I grew it in November when things started to get cold."

"You would be chilled without it now," I said.

"Damn right I would!"

His trailer and horses moved down the paved road with the timelessness of a man who is comfortable in his own lifestyle. I moved down the road a short way and gazed at deep ruts cutting across the grassy hills to the south. Horse-drawn wagons had gone here too. They were the tracks of Custer's expedition of 1874.

CHAPTER 12

WILD HORSE HARRY HARDIN AND POKER ALICE

There are two towns in Keystone: a new one to sell souvenirs, gasoline, meals, and tourist aids that is open only five months a year, and Old Keystone, built on the side of the Holy Terror Mine. Old Keystone has a general store and other services that are open all year. If it seems less picturesque than new Keystone, it is because the colors are more subdued. It was built to live in, not to impress people.

A white bearded man was loading groceries into a saddlebag outside the general store. He was just the man I was looking for — Wild Horse Harry Hardin. I asked him if we could talk, and he said sure; as soon as he got his groceries put away, we could go down to the saloon and he would have plenty of time to talk.

It was an incongruous sight. Harry scraped his horse's droppings off the blacktop road into a cardboard box and deposited them in a litter can. Then he sat tall in the saddle while the horse's hooves clattered down the street of Keystone to the bar.

We sat in a quiet corner. I sipped coke while Harry reminisced and sipped his favorite drink. Harry was 83 when I visited him. He had been in Keystone since 1922.

"I rode with the Texas Rangers for three years. I was 17 and 160 pounds then, and my job was to patrol the Mexican border. It was during the Tong Wars and the Chinese was coming into Mexico at $100 a head, and then they was dumped in the U.S."

Tongs were clannish fraternal organizations that ruled Chinese communities. For seemingly inexplicable reasons the clans would go to war with one another. These battles often reflected conditions in the homeland, but could also be local in origin.

Deadwood became the last Chinatown and held many laundries, restaurants, opium dens, and brothels.

There were Tongs in Deadwood, but I could find no record of Tong battles.

During Harry's time on the Mexican border the Chinese homeland had just undergone a rebellion which replaced the Manchu Dynasty with Sun Yat-Sen and a host of provincial warlords. Unscrupulous sailors made money by taking Chinese from their homeland and dumping them at accessible ports, like Mexico's.

"I got shot at a few times, but mainly I got lonesome. I quit the Rangers and went back to Amarillo. I was tired of desert and cactus and went home to visit my folks. Then I caught on with Buffalo Bill. Now there's some guy. Bill was the nicest guy you ever met. He was so generous he would give money to anyone who asked for it and he never told a lie!

"I rode broncs for three years for the Wild West Show. We played in the New York City Gardens, and St. Louis, and Omaha, and just about every big city around. We traveled at night in private railroad cars. There were 1100 people all together.

"Then in 1908 Bill went to England, and I left the show and went to Oklahoma where I got a job busting broncs for the Miller Brothers 101 Show. They had a 101,000 acre spread.

"I saw my father in Ponco City, Oklahoma, and went to Amarillo again to stay with my sister. I heard there was lots of open country yet up in the Dakotas, so I saddled a horse and rode north. Nine weeks later I was in the Black Hills. I stayed in cowboy camps or range camps all the way. It didn't cost me anything. The night watch would ask who you were and what you wanted and then ride you into camp. Course he had a gun on you. There was still rustlers around. But once you squared things, there was hot grub and good company.

"I only paid for things once. I stayed with a Swede and in the morning I asked him, 'What do I owe you?'"

"He thought and then said, 'Well, I tell you, you had a plenty good dinner, a nice bed, and a good breakfast, and your horse had a good feeding, so how's about 35 cents?' Well, I gave him $5 and rode off. I had $700 in my saddlebags.

"I got to Keystone and staked eight claims of 20 acres each. When I ran out of money, I lived with the Indians on Pine Ridge and caught and broke wild horses. My wife was a squaw, Spanish and Sioux, and we stayed with her people until I could sell enough horses to cowboys and the army to stake me.

"I mined for twelve years and I made $2100 a week for twelve years, then I sold out for $60,000. I had the Golden Eagle, Eagle, and a bunch of others. I built a home right across the street, there."

He gestured out the window at a brown frame house across the street from the bar. Then he stroked his long white beard and settled into thought again.

"Bought that lot for $17 and kept my folks there for 12 years. My mother died, and I gave the house to Dad. He sold it.

"After the war the government froze out all the small miners. They would only buy from corporations like Homestake, not individuals. I bought a donkey, went on the streets, let kids sit on it, let folks take photos, and I would take donations. I just finished my fifteenth year.

"One year I went to California to visit my brother, and I got in to some movies. We went to Paramount with my folks and got a guide to take us around. Well, it turned out that the guide used to be a foreman on a ranch in Wyoming. 'You ever been in Wyoming?' he says. 'Yup,' I says, 'The 33 Bar Ranch.' 'Well, I'll be. Do you remember when you were repairing fence one day and I was on the other side working for the next ranch? You said you would never do that job again and I offered you a job. Do you remember?' 'I sure do.' 'Say, can you rope a cow, and jump through a loop like you used to?' 'Yup!'

"Well, he ran into a room and came out with a real good rope. I made the loop, jumped in and out, and then lassoed this old foreman around the neck. He got excited and tells me he is going to get someone else to see me, and he wants me to do exactly the same thing. Afterwards he tells me who he is, says his rope artist is sick, and they have a picture they want to finish. 'Can you ride a horse?' 'Yup!'

"He offered me $100 a week, and I ended up being in five movies: **1880 Train, Tomahawk, How the West Was Won, Last of the Buffalo Herd**, and **The Home of the Cowboy**."

I asked him how he got started with a donkey on the street after leading an adventurous life like his.

"There was a guy on the streets with goats and a little cart. Kids would ride in the cart, and the people would go crazy over it. He says to me, 'Why don't you get something too?' 'What would I get?' I asked him. And he said, 'A donkey, people go for that.'

"Well I didn't go right out and get one, but one day I was offered a donkey and bought it. The first time I came into town with it, a guy asks if his kid can sit on it. Sure, I says, and the next thing I know cameras are everywhere. I knew then that I was in business."

I asked him what Keystone had been like.

"Keystone wore out. It had three saloons, a grocery, meat market, bank, blacksmith, and livery. There was fights every night. Most people worked in the Holy Terror Mine. Then in '42 it was closed down, and the miners were moved to get copper for the war. Only the Homestake could get money to reopen."

I was curious about what he did when the tourist season was over.

"I still pan a little, but mostly I hunt and fish and write poetry. I write it in my head. You want to hear one?"

His poem was about a club that struck in the night with the power of death. The mood was suspenseful as the club raised and fell. The club struck, and the victim of the attack turned out to be a potato bug. Harry laughed, his eyes twinkled, and he stroked his beard.

The reminiscences were scattered now as he remembered the people he had met. He worked for two weeks on Rushmore, but got fired for taking two days off to hunt. He insists that Borglum had promised him the time, but that the temperamental artist could forget things like that.

"John Wesley Hardin was my great uncle. He built the town of Hardin, Montana, and they named a county after him. Then he robbed a bank just for a lark. He didn't need the money, and they shot him.

"I used to take my donkey to Deadwood and walk in the 'Days of '76' parade with Potato Creek Johnny. I've had three donkeys. Billy the Kid was my first; he died of old age. Sunshine died in the flood of '72, and Sugar Baby is my current donkey.

"Poker Alice died in 1930. She was a good friend and the best card shark that ever turned a card. She could read the back of a card as easy as she could read the face, and they weren't marked. She showed me a few tricks. There was always a cigar in her mouth. If it went out, she'd just chew it.

"Some guy insulted her daughter, so she shot him and called the sheriff to come and get the body. Believe me, from then on no one bothered that girl. Morning came and she strapped on the gunbelt as regular as putting on shoes. At night, it hung on her bedpost.

"Poker Alice wasn't always a gambler, but her luck with husbands was not as good as her luck with cards. When her first husband died, she needed money to live on. Where could a woman make money in a town with one or two stores and a row of saloons and bars? There was one possibility. Her husband Frank had taught her how to play poker, and she had always been very lucky. She tried her skills and found that her husband had not just been letting her win. She moved from one gambling community to another until she settled in at Deadwood to be their best Faro dealer."

Faro was a gambling game only. There was very little room for skill and strategy, but that didn't keep it from being the most popular game in the United States during this era. Faro terms like "coppering the bet" and "calling the turn" were part of the American idioms.

The first card in a deck was the "soda" and the last was the "hock." The table had a cloth with a betting arrangement for chips, and the dealer controlled the cards which were turned over one at a time. The players bet on which card would come up second. The first card lost; chips on that number were collected by the dealer. If there were chips on the second card, they won. Every other card was a winner. Bets were left, moved, and lost while the deck dwindled. Then at the end of the deck, the players had new betting options. Furious activity centered around the loser, winner, and "hock" cards.

The dealer had a Faro case that looked like a gambler's abacus. In the middle of the case were two rows

designating the 13 kinds of cards in a deck; each card had a post with four markers on it. Winning and losing cards were recorded with the abacus markers. Like "Blackjack," the odds improved as the deck was played through. It was an easy way to lose everything.

"Alice married a gambler named Tubbs and worked the tables until her beauty left and her lifestyle lost its charm. Then she and Tubbs retired to a ranch. Tubbs died of pneumonia during a blizzard. Poker Alice had to ride 40 miles after the storm subsided to get two men to bury him. They wanted $25 to do the job and Alice had no money, so she took her diamond into a store and hocked it for the money. She asked if she could deal at a local Faro table 'just so I can get $25.' It took her an hour and a half, and she was good to her word. She left, redeemed her ring, and went back to their cabin.

"Well, she stayed there for three months, and it got too lonesome for her. She came into Sturgis, set up a Faro game, gambled, bought a house, and hired some girls."

Harry chuckled, stretched his foot-long beard, and leaned forward.

"She never let them girls work on Sunday. She even had Sunday School lessons for them. Fellows could come anytime of day or night, she would never let one in on Sunday."

Each Black Hills town had its own character, and the uniqueness of the individual infused life into the memory of gold miners and spilled whiskey. For Keystone that special quality comes from Wild Horse Harry.

CHAPTER 13

Bob Brislawn and the Sundance Kid

On my way into the town of Sundance I picked up a brochure that proclaimed, "The Sundance Kid Was Here." Was Harry Longabaugh born here? Did the Sundance Kid terrorize the town with Butch Cassidy and Kid Curry? In the city museum I found a courthouse replica depicting the setting for the trial of the Sundance Kid. I began to search for the story behind it.

Harry Longabaugh, the Sundance Kid, was a 19-year-old ex-cowpuncher when he turned outlaw. He had been employed by one of the best outfits in Montana when

he got fired and had to seek other ways of making his fortune.

The Black Hills beckoned with gold and silver lining the streams and, more importantly, lining pants' pockets. Harry turned outlaw and made his first robbery on Crow Creek. His first theft was a six-shooter, horse, saddle, bridle, and chaps. Now he was outfitted for his next robberies.

This particular robbery took place southeast of Sundance, and it was Sheriff Ryan's job to chase down the desperado. This took the sheriff 200 miles away to Montana in one of the biggest merry-go-round adventures of the west. The initial capture was no problem, but the trail he took back to Sundance's courtroom was legendary in itself.

Ordinarily, the sheriff would have returned by stage to Spearfish and then by horseback — or by horseback all the way; but this time Ryan decided to return by train. This doesn't sound too ridiculous until you check the railroad routes and find that the train from Miles City, Montana, went to St. Paul, Minnesota, where Sheriff Ryan had to catch another train to the Black Hills, a route of approximately 2,000 miles.

This return trip turned out to be even longer for Harry Longabaugh because he escaped near Duluth and took the Canadian Pacific back to Montana. He stole seven head of horses from an operator in Canada, stole one horse from the Crow Reservation, one horse from the Beasley and Newman sheep ranch, and still another one from the Liscom Ranch. Sheriff Davis caught the horse trader in Montana and wired Sheriff Ryan. This time Ryan and Longabaugh returned by the Miles City-Deadwood stagecoach.

On August 5th the outlaw was sentenced to prison, had his head and beard shaved, and was locked up in the Sundance jail. The state penitentiary was full, so Harry remained in the local calaboose until February 5, 1889, at which time he was pardoned. He left Sundance and never returned.

As a souvenir he took the town's name and went on to bigger adventures with Butch Cassidy. The final Black Hills episode for the Kid was in 1897 when he and Butch robbed the bank at Belle Fourche. They were put into the local jail, but it burned down, and they were transferred to the Deadwood jail. This was the beginning of their notorious careers, not the end, and the name Sundance went on to stand for a gunslinger more than for a town.

Fame changes things. Here is a town located at the foot of Wi Wacippi Paha, the temple of the Sioux, where the sacred sun dance was held, yet its fame stemmed from a charge of grand larceny.

The museum revealed another character to learn about, one who gave the region something to be proud of. His name was Bob Brislawn.

Bob was a genuine frontier character. He wore a cowboy's vest and chaps, a ten-gallon hat, and a kerchief tied around his neck. He was a small man with sandy hair, a golden mustache, and a broad smile, who worked for the United States Topographic Survey from 1911 through the 1930's as a packer and a teamster. Quietly these men surveyed the rugged mountains and dry deserts of the west, filling in the blanks of half an unexplored continent.

The Topographic Survey was a map and transit team that measured and recorded everything on the landscape, regardless of the difficulty of the terrain. The surveyors were dependent on men like Brislawn to get their equipment to the job, and Bob's job was dependent on good animals. Lame animals meant hardship and inefficiency, so Bob was part veterinarian and part pal to each animal. He was a master trainer and healer with a St. Francis of Assisi touch for all animals.

Part of the job of caring for animals is choosing the right animal for a job. Brislawn chose the Spanish mustang, or Barb horses, for his pack carriers. They were smaller than most horse breeds, seventeen ribs instead of eighteen.

Brislawn's survey chiefs were John Blackburn and T. F. Murphy. During his career with them he was in every mountain state in the west. He had the first horses on top of the mountains in Colorado, two Spanish mustangs that carried the survey instruments above treeline. Before he stopped surveying, he said, "I forded every river and swam horses across every river and climbed every hill from the Mexican border to the Canadian line."

His chief would say of him, "Take Bob, he can cook, ride, map, and record; and he's got a string of pack horses that can go where a mountain goat can't."

In 1916 Bob managed to homestead the Cayuse Ranch near Oshota, west of Devils Tower. He married Genevieve Irwin, a school teacher from the logging town of Hullett in 1930. Thirteen years later she died, leaving him with five children to raise.

With the help of his brother Ferdinande, he not only raised his children, but he also sought to preserve the Spanish mustang that was now being shot and sold for dog food. In the early 1930's most people thought the Spanish mustang was an animal of history, but somehow Bob did the impossible and saved them. Bob Brislawn — Mr. Mustang, The Wyoming Kid — who had founded the Spanish Mustang Registry, Inc. in 1957 so that his life work could go on, died at Moorcroft in 1979.

CHAPTER 14 # DEADWOOD

I drove into Deadwood expecting wooden sidewalks and horses. I wanted to see the Chinese section where 106 Chinese migrants were establishing their culture in a reckless mining town.

The **Deadwood Pioneer Times** had this account:

Among their number was a beautiful young girl named Yellow Doll, who lived in a luxurious setting. None knew if she was slave or princess. She wore handsome clothes and beautiful jewelry, but she was not loved by the dance hall girls who dubbed her 'that slant-eyed come-on.' Mystery surrounded her in life — and in death. She was brutally murdered. A hatchet was the weapon. The murderer never was found, nor was the reason ever discovered.

The leading Chinese gave her an elaborate funeral . . . It is not known where Yellow Doll was buried, or if her bones later were disinterred and removed to the land of her ancestors as were other Chinese buried in the gulch.

I wanted to see the site of that heinous murder. But I couldn't find the early false front stores or the miners shanties. At first I thought the city had done the worst — torn them down. But then I learned that there is no original Deadwood any more. In fact, nature has made sure that Deadwood gets a facelift every few years. The early town was a crowded, unruly settlement, with tents pitched in the middle of muddy streets, and bullwhackers and riders pushing between canvas and people.

It was a time of daily suicides and regular homicides, alcohol and starvation. Even in the midst of boom there was bust among the starving crowds. Claim offices, saloons, and stores sprang up overnight and seldom waited for completion before opening. The main street was barely tacked together. Fires were regular events as people struggled to keep warm and survive. Each day saw a flow of people in and a flow of people out. Dreamers replaced the disillusioned, and Deadwood began to take shape.

The **Black Hills Pioneer** had the following description of the community in 1876:

The Deadwood Country

We do not believe this or any other country affords such another example of rapid development as what is now known as 'The Deadwood Country.' Three months ago it was occupied by only a few hardy miners — scarce fifty in

number — who had placed their lives in peril, both from Indians and starvation, living on 'meat straight', without even salt, for months, and undergoing nearly every privation known to man in search of the precious metal. Now Deadwood, Whitewood, and their tributaries, are peopled by more than seven thousand of as hardy, energetic and intelligent men as there are in the country; men who have left home, wife, and children, and endured hardships and incurred dangers that those in the States little dream of, in search of a better country — more money. They have found it, and today, go where you will, the sound of the pick, shovel, rocker, and sledge greets your ear, and sluice-boxes, ditches and dams are on every hand.

Six weeks ago the site of Deadwood City was a heavy forest of pine timber; now it extends nearly a mile along Deadwood and Whitewood, and contains nearly two thousand of the most energetic, driving people on the continent. Every branch of business is represented, and many of them are overdone. Houses are going up on every hand — immense trains are constantly arriving loaded with goods of all kinds, business is rushing, and bargains are driven here that would put Wall Street to blush. In addition to Deadwood, Montana City, Centennial and Spearfish have sprung into existence, and each and all are growing rapidly.

Let the Government but protect this people and give them mail facilities, and within two years the Black Hills will contain more than 200,000 of prosperous and happy souls. We know that the country is wonderfully rich in its mines of gold, silver, and other minerals, in its vast forests of pine and in its grazing and agricultural resources.

The Black Hills are a success — complete, entire, in spite of rival mining districts, 'croakers,' 'tender-feet,' and barbarous Indians. Let those who have found the fight and won the battle work together patiently, earnestly, unitedly. We have full faith that the government will soon come to our assistance — extend a helping hand, and throw around us its strong arm of protection and welcome us as no longer outlaws. May God in His providence speed the day.

A major flood swept through the valley in 1878 and washed away the rubble.

In January of 1879 the same newspaper reported,

Deadwood, the metropolis of the Black Hills, contains 6,000 inhabitants, 500 business firms, churches, schools, and numerous secret organizations.

This frontier town was so bustling that they even had their own theater, managed by Jack Langrishe. After leaving a wake of bad debts in Cheyenne and other mining towns, Langrishe found success in Deadwood. In his canvas-roofed theater he offered "Lillian's Lost Love or The Banker's Daughter" and other classics to the rowdy inhabitants of the gold borough.

The Bella Union Theatre and the 500 business firms could not withstand the combination of spot fires and the devastation of major disasters. In 1879 fire ran down the streets like a miner who had just made the big strike. In 1881 a tornado came into town; in 1883, a flood; in 1959, another fire; and in 1965, the worst flood ever. I could not see the Deadwood I wanted to see because it was not there.

What I could find was the spirit of Deadwood's glory years. The bar names, the street names, everything in Deadwood seemed to cling to the nebulous ghosts of the boom years. The town could do a better job of being Old Deadwood in a physical sense, but nothing has diminished the essence of its wild west days when this was the place of frontier legends.

Tombstone, Dodge City, Virginia City, and Abilene had each been the epitome of the golden west, but Deadwood came when the era seemed to be dying out and gave it another gasp of life. Maybe that is why old gunmen like Doc Holliday, Wyatt Earp, and Bat Masterson made appearances here. It was almost the end of the era of the pistol, but at its zenith the shootist had quite a hold on Deadwood. Much of the image is pure fiction, and many of the true incidents have been embellished, but I doubt if very many people care. They are more interested in being where Wild Bill Hickok, Calamity Jane, and Preacher Smith once walked.

CHAPTER 15

WILD BILL HICKOK, CALAMITY JANE, AND PREACHER SMITH

People in Deadwood lined up along main street an hour early to get a view of the pageant of the shooting of Wild Bill Hickok and the trial of Jack McCall. What was it that made Hickok and the others bigger than life? Why did people flock to this nightly recreation?

Wild Bill came to Deadwood with his career behind him. He had been successful as a lawman in Hayes City and Abilene, and he had adorned the New York stage with Buffalo Bill. Now, with a wife waiting in St. Louis, the aging gunman with failing eyesight wandered into the pandemonium of the Deadwood valley to seek his fortune.

The gulch was made up of three camps — Elizabeth City, Crook City, and Deadwood which was located at the head of the gulch and, therefore, was the most prominent. Hickok led his wagon train down the snaking roadway between tree stumps and potholes. The street was packed with jostling men, horses, mules, oxen, wagons, coaches, and carts. The tall man wearing a Prince Albert frock coat, checkered trousers, cape, and two revolvers with their butts forward, was probably lost in the crowd.

On a box in front of Bent and Deetken's Drugstore he might have heard the oration of a six-foot, lean, black bearded man called Preacher Smith, a New England sky pilot whose full name was Henry Weston Smith. He was the antithesis of Hickok, a quiet, conservative man trying to attract a crowd.

In March of 1876 Smith joined a party of gold hunters in Louisville and followed them to Custer, South Dakota, where his interest was in the saving of souls, not searching for yellow metal. George Ayres recorded the following diary note about Smith's stay in Custer:

May 7: Rev. Smith held the first church services in the Hills. Congregation composed of thirty men and five women. I attended. He took his text from Psalm 34:7, and preached a very interesting sermon. The congregation paid strict attention to the sermon except when there was a dog fight outside.

The Bible verse reads, "The angel of the Lord encampeth round about them that fear him, and he delivereth them." These words were probably very significant to people who had anything but angels camped around them each day.

When gold was found in Deadwood, Custer was deserted, and Preacher Smith followed the wave of men by arranging a ride with the former army scout and good friend of Wild Bill Hickok, Captain Gardner. Being a prolific writer, Gardner recorded this episode on their three-day journey to Deadwood:

We made our first camp near Hill City, and hardly got the team unhitched until our passenger had a fire built and

74

water provided for the evening meal. When ready, our guest was absent. I looked around and found him sitting on a log a few rods distant, reading. I went to him, and to my surprise found him reading a Bible. After a few words with him, he told me he was a Methodist preacher. I remarked that I thought he was up against a hard proposition. He said, 'Possibly so, but I will do the best I can'."

Among the hard propositions were Hickok's friends, California Joe and Colorado Charlie Utter. These men were former army scouts with Bill, and each was seeking his own fortune in The Hills. Charlie put together an idea for a pony express to Deadwood. He also indulged in the startling habit of bathing every morning. It was such a unique habit that he regularly drew a crowd.

To gain a stake for himself and his new wife, Hickok could choose among these: the gold fields with hard work, big odds and claim jumpers; an offer to join Charlie Utter in the pony express venture; gambling in the numerous saloons; and even the remote possibility of pinning on a badge again to clean out killers like Charlie Storms and Jim Levy who were terrorizing the town. Hickok chose to gamble.

To provide for his needs, Preacher Smith worked at manual labor during the weekdays. He cut timber, constructed cabins, and worked as a fireman in a sawmill. From this he sustained himself and sent money to his family. On Sundays he preached.

An acquaintance of both Bill and Preacher Smith was Calamity Jane who is reputed to have been raised by the soldiers in Fort Laramie, an orphan of a former comrade who married and left the cavalry only to be killed by Indians. She wore two Colt revolvers and carried a bullwhip.

It is evident that what the soldiers taught Calamity did not include how to be a lady. She was tougher than most of the men, could swear better than they could, and could outgamble and outshoot them. She had been a stowaway in the Jenny-Dodge expedition, masquerading as a soldier until she was caught halfway to The Hills. Her experience made her a good scout for Wild Bill's wagon train.

She also drove stage and was reputed to be one of the best bullwhackers in the west. A bull team consisted of seven or eight yoke of oxen hitched to an old Murphy or Kern wagon and then loaded with 7500-8000 pounds. In order to keep teams moving, a bullwhacker used abusive language and a bullwhip. The profanity was mostly for passing ears while the crack of the whip just above the oxen's shoulders was like a shot during a battle with a mudhole or other obstacle. The sound spurred the oxen on.

The freighters often traveled in teams. The combined outfit was led by a wagon boss who patrolled the train, set the pace, and scouted for stream-fords and campsites. His assistant rode near the end of the train where newer drivers were assigned. Here he could watch the mess wagon, the calf yard, and the herders. Each bullwhacker walked to the left side of the team between the first and second rank of oxen.

Calamity Jane was famous as a female bullwhacker. Her fame was not based just on her bravado with the whip and ox-team. She was an adventuress in an age when suffragettes were just beginning to whisper in backrooms. By 1890 only four states gave women the right to vote, yet Calamity Jane could get into bars where Poker Alice was kept out.

According to some records, Wild Bill and Calamity fell in love and married. Since Hickok was already married, this seems doubtful even in those bawdy times. It does seem likely that they spent some time together, at least at the poker table. Jane liked to talk of their romance. She was building a reputation as a wild woman, and she encouraged any rumor that added to that prestige.

To the aging Hickok, it was the end of the line, and like so many gunslingers, he became a fatalist. On a ride with Charlie Utter he once said, "Charlie, I feel this is going to be my last camp, and I won't leave it alive." He also expressed his gloom in a letter to his wife:

Agnes Darling, if such should be we never meet again, while firing my last shot, I will gently breathe the name of my wife — Agnes — and with wishes for my enemies I will make the plunge and try to swim to the other shore.

On August 1, 1876, Hickok sat in on several poker games, always taking a chair that kept his back to the wall. This was a right he was never refused. During the session a man named Jack McCall sat in and lost all his money. Wild Bill gave McCall money for supper and made his way back to camp. He should have known that no man likes charity, even when he needs it.

August 2, 1876, was destined to be Deadwood's most famous day. Just two months after his arrival, the fastest gun in the west was dead.

Wearing his favorite outfit, Hickok had wandered into Nuttall and Mann's No. 10 in the early afternoon. The sheriff, a steamboat captain, and a friend had invited Bill to join them in a game. He sat down without his back to the wall. The front door swung open, and Jack McCall entered. He stared around the room and slipped to the bar behind Bill. He stopped and watched.

Bill kiddingly disputed with a player named Massie. "The old duffer — he broke me on the hand."

McCall stood nervously, but no one paid any attention to him, particularly Bill who was now intent upon his new hand — two black aces, two black eights, and the jack of diamonds.

A shot shattered the buzz of barroom milling.

"Damn you, take that!", yelled McCall, his pistol

smoking. Captain Massie felt a numbness in his left wrist and stared at the gunman. As he did, Hickok silently fell to the floor, dead. The ball had passed through Bill's head and into Massie's wrist.

McCall pulled the trigger twice more, aiming at George Shingle and Harry Young; but the gun misfired, and McCall ran out the back door. A horse was tied there, and he jumped on it; but the owner had loosened the saddle, and the chagrined killer rolled under the belly of the startled animal. Gasping for breath, McCall got to his feet and ran.

"WILD BILL IS SHOT! WILD BILL IS SHOT!"

McCall tried to hide in a butcher shop, but a Sharp's rifle dissuaded him. He was caught.

McCall seemed destined for the gallows when a Mexican rider came into town carrying an Indian's head. The town toasted and rewarded him and forgot McCall. According to one tale, the Mexican was shot later that day for refusing to show the Indian head without a payment. Some men set out for Crook City to get more Indians.

In the furor, Judge Kuykendall convened a court of townsmen who were tired, perhaps drunk, and certainly disinterested. They made the trial short. When McCall said that Hickok had shot his brother, the court said that justified his action and let him go.

Calamity Jane claimed to have tracked McCall to Yankton, South Dakota, where a real judge and jury found it hard to believe that McCall's brother, who was still walking around, could have been a victim of Hickok. They hung McCall and called the Deadwood trial an illegal court. Few people, including Mrs. Hickok, would buy that version. Calamity Jane wanted the glory of catching McCall, but her part in the story was complete fabrication. Her real role in the episode would never be known.

Charlie Utter was running a pony express race to establish his freight company, a race he ran in record time. By the time Colorado Charlie arrived, the events of the day had gotten out of hand. He must have wondered where all the cheering crowds had gone.

California Joe went to McCall's place and called him out. McCall didn't draw, and California Joe wouldn't murder him. A lynch party was organized and failed: McCall sensed the danger in the air and left.

Colonel May, the prosecutor, was the one who finally got McCall brought to justice. After the trial he swore that there would be justice, and he was the one who got the warrant served in Yankton.

Calamity Jane was always looking for people to associate with, especially colorful people, and she decided that Preacher Smith was a good target. She claimed to have been affected by Henry Smith's ministry. Whether she was or not cannot be proven, but her association with him wasn't much longer than that with Hickok. On August 20 Preacher Smith held services in Deadwood, then began his walk to Crook City. On his cabin door he left a note, "Gone to Crook City and if God is willing, be back at 2 PM." He never took a gun, for his Bible was his protection.

That afternoon his body was found halfway to Crook City with a rifle bullet in his breast. Some said Indians, some said outlaws. The fact was that he was dead. His body was brought back to Deadwood and buried in Boot Hill near Hickok's grave. Calamity Jane claimed to have prepared his body for burial. Upstanding citizens took offense. No one really knows.

For Jane, the minister's words may have made a difference or her rough exterior may have been a long-time coverup. That same month Deadwood was ravaged with a smallpox epidemic. She was the community's most active nurse. Many people owed their lives to Calamity's care.

In various books authors tell of Jane's demise, her life as an alcoholic, and her loss of beauty and vigor. They tell of her death of pneumonia in 1903 and of her request to be buried next to Wild Bill, a request that was granted to her.

I prefer to think of her as **Calamity Jane, The Heroine of Whoop-up**, in the Deadwood Dick Library, or as she is in the 1887 biography, **Calamity Jane, A Story of the Black Hills**:

She's a wild 'un! Man or ooman? Who ken tell? Wi' the face o' a girl, an' the strength o' a man, an' more darin' than both on 'em tergither. But no badness in her, no meanness. That Calamity! Here's one fer her!"

CHAPTER 16 THE HEROES OF DEADWOOD

As I lay beneath the big dipper and fingered my **Beadle Pocket Library Book, Wild Bill, The Pistol Prince,** I wondered how many people had been lost in the legend of Wild Bill. Who were the desperadoes and lawmen that had been buried and forgotten behind the image of the "Deadman's Hand?"

I read, "But Bill had been twice slightly wounded, one of his horses was shot in the neck, and in the stage, which had been fairly riddled with arrows, many of which still stuck in it, lay three dead men, passengers, while the other two did not escape scathless.

"Back at the still pursuing red-skins Bill opened with his rifle as the stage team, nearly tired out, climbed the hill, and thus kept them at bay until a party of mounted men, hearing the firing, came out from the station and put them to flight." And then I fell asleep.

Fresh air and warm nights will snatch alertness and let sleep in quickly. I must have dozed for a considerable time and then driven into Deadwood in a daze because I don't remember coming into the No. 10 Saloon and ordering a coke, but here I sat in the fogginess of too many cigars and cigarettes with a mustachioed miner sitting across the table from me.

In the smoke his features were hazy. He was wearing a wool plaid coat over a western style shirt, and his wide-brimmed hat rested on the table beside his drink. His age had worn his features but could not mask the fact that he must have been a dashing figure in the past. Not wanting to seem too out of it, I decided to engage him in conversation, but was interrupted when a large man with a Stetson bellowed,

"I coppered the Queen! He moved my chip!"

The Faro dealer was a small man. He stood beside his casekeeper and looked nonplussed by the commotion.

"Last turn."

"Cases on the King!" someone called.

"I was cheated!"

The man in the Stetson grabbed the dealer. The dealer lashed out with a short, quick hand, and the Stetson crumbled over the green felt tablecloth.

My partner chuckled while the big man was carried out.

"Reminds me of Luke Short," he said.

That was my chance. He had started the conversation. I didn't have to sound like a drowsy dolt.

"Who reminds you of Luke Short?"

"The small guy dealing Faro. Luke was a dealer in the Oriental down in Tombstone. Bat Masterson and Wyatt Earp were dealers too, but they had a reputation and Luke didn't. So Charlie Storms, a bad man from Deadwood, hits Tombstone and wants to make his mark. He joins a group of gamblers that wanted to take over the Oriental and he figures Luke would be easy pickings to begin with.

"He comes into the saloon all liquored up and Deadwood nasty, and says to his friend, 'That little one there? A fighter?'

"After a stiff drink he faces Luke again. 'I never seen no Rickenbaugh gambler who wouldn't cheat his own grandma.'

"Luke did nothing. Storms was enraged and accused Luke of being yellow. Luke did nothing but play on.

"'Damn you, Short, you're asking for it!'

"Masterson walked the frustrated Storms out of the casino. Storms waited outside for Luke. When Luke appeared, he walked straight at Charlie without a flinch. The big man got flustered, drew, and fired wildly. Luke drew, aimed, and put three lethal slugs in Charlie."

"Who were the other bad men of this area?"

"Jim Levy was a Deadwood gunny. Right after he arrived in Cheyenne from Deadwood, he got into an argument with Charlie Harrison at Bowlby's Gambling Saloon. They yelled and screamed until their necks swelled with veins near bursting, and then they both ran to get their hardware.

"Well, the west wasn't filled with as many of them gunfights on main street as the old movies tried to claim, but here was a classic confrontation. Harrison was well-known and favored, but Deadwood is a tough training ground. Charlie filled the air with lead and smoke. Jim shot once and walked away."

I had my coke glass refilled, grabbed a few pretzels, and settled in.

"So many of these tales seem to happen in places besides Deadwood," I said. "Didn't anything happen here?"

"Well, there was Turkey Creek Jack Johnson's gun battle. He was a gambler working the saloons in the gulch. One night in 1876 he got in this row with two gunnies and invited them both to a shootout at the cemetery.

"Well, the three of them met along one fence of the graveyard. Each of the gunmen had two revolvers. Johnson stood at one end of the fence; they stood side by side at the other. At fifty yards the two of 'em cleared leather and sent lead flying. Johnson's Colt stayed in the holster.

"In ten yards they had one empty gun each. At thirty yards Johnson shot once, and one fell dead. The second man hurried two, three quick shots. Johnson took a few more steps and fired a second shot. It was all over. Turkey Creek had known the distances of the fence and his gun. He had won his biggest gamble.

"Course you got to remember that the west wasn't exactly a blue collar district. Them miners that sweated and worked long hours didn't have time to make the headlines and them that did raise hell had to keep moving to avoid the noose.

"As a matter of fact, one of the most famous desperadoes in the west got started here and never came back. Sam Bass was known as a Texas Terror back in the 1880's, but I'll tell you this, it was Deadwood that broke him in.

"He and his partner Joel Collins had just come up from Texas with a trail herd of rustled beef that they sold in Oglalla, Nebraska, when they heard word of the big strike in Deadwood. It was really busting loose about this time, and he and Joel came here with fresh dollars and lots of ideas.

"Then the thermometer hit 30 below zero and wouldn't budge. By this time the boys' bucks ran out, their gold hadn't come in, their efforts to gamble and to run a bordello had failed, and the snows were replaced with knee-deep mud. Sam and Joel were busted.

"'Hell, let's bust a stage!' Sam declared.

"Sam's solution made sense to Joel and to Billy Reddy, Frank Towle, and Jim Berry. They stole some horses and waylaid Johnny Slaughter's rig three miles out of town. Johnny was a popular figure in these parts, and he was mighty brave too. Voorhees had assigned him to the dangerous mountain division because he considered him his most dependable six-horse driver.

"Well, Johnny pulled to a stop and did what he was told, but Bill Reddy blasted him with a shotgun anyway. The horses panicked and took off with the $15,000 strongbox intact. They ran all the way to Deadwood, leaving the Bass-Collins group frustrated. Sam threatened to kill Reddy, who took off and was never heard from again. Sam took off to the south where he waged war with the Union Pacific. Meanwhile, Deadwood held a funeral for Slaughter at the Grand Central Hotel, and both men and women were part of the large turnout. The stage carried lots of money from the gold field so it was an attractive temptation to lots of bad men."

"What about lawmen?" I asked. "Hickok was a former sheriff, and Bat Masterson and Wyatt Earp were too. Did any of them put on a badge here?"

The old man wrapped his weathered hands around his glass, took a short quick drink, and stared into the street past the bat-winged doors.

"Nope, none of them wore a star here. But we had Seth Bullock."

"I never heard of him. Did he ever do anything special?"

The old man's eyes turned to me and burned into my mind.

"He stayed alive and enforced the law in Deadwood. Seems to me that's pretty special. Seth was a former Rough Rider with Teddy Roosevelt. He was also part of TR's inaugural parade with a bunch of local cowboys. But his contribution to this area was his honesty as a marshal. I can picture him yet, black bowler hat set back on his head, dark heavy eyebrows that seemed to make his eyes look like they were inches deep in his skull, and a bushy mustache that swept out across each cheek and hid his upper lip. He was tall, thin, and strong; and his eyes could cut right through a man.

"He was a sheriff in Montana before he came to Deadwood. He even introduced a resolution in Congress to set aside Yellowstone as a National Park while a member of the Territorial Senate. He had been to Yellowstone on an early expedition. The gold lure was strong for this adventurer, like it had been for so many. He sent his wife and daughter to Michigan, and he came to the gulch. With a friend, Sol Star, he arranged to take a load of hardware to Deadwood and set up a business.

"At this time claim jumpers were running rampant. The miners were armed, and One-eyed McTigue organized them to fight the jumpers. A black miner named Posey struck a good claim at Nigger Hill. Crazy Horse was camped near Devils Tower, and Wild Bill was in town. The month before Jack Hinch was killed by another miner, Jerry McCarty, in Grayville. James Shannon and Tom Moore had a fist fight that ended in an agreement to shoot on sight. Shannon was killed, and because of the agreement Moore was released.

The foreman of the jury stated, 'The killing was done according to Hoyle and what he says goes in that town.'

"The day after Bullock arrived, Hickok was shot. A smallpox epidemic that the doctor had first diagnosed as poison ivy struck next. Then in late August a bartender named Sam Young was arrested for shooting a vagrant. At the trial Seth was selected as sheriff, his first commission in Deadwood. Young was released since the bum reminded him of Laughing Sam who had threatened to kill Sam Young. Crazy Horse raided a Montana herd near Deadwood on August 20, and Preacher Smith was killed the same day. The town was in need of law and order, and Seth Bullock was the man they turned to. His first job was to tell Wyatt Earp that the job was no longer up for grabs. From then on he ran the sheriff's office with an efficiency that was not part of many old west lawmen.

"By November, 1877, Bullock had established his reputation and made many arrests. He had also stopped a jailbreak, but it was at the Keets Mine that his reputation was really made. Thirty miners had seized the mine to demand back pay. They holed up at the mine with an adequate supply of food and water, and they defied the law to come and get them. A frontal assault wouldn't do for all the miners were all well-armed. Everything seemed to point to lots of bloodshed, an outcome Bullock didn't like. Then he got an inspiration. He got sulphur from the laundry of his friend Wing Suey and lowered burning sulphur down the mine shaft. The results were quick and inevitable, and no blood was lost."

I was so absorbed in his tales that I didn't want him to stop. "There doesn't seem to be any end to the heroes of this valley. Who would you say was the most unusual?"

"That's easy — Buster the dog."

"You've got to tell me that story."

His face wrinkled as the corners of his mouth turned up, and he leaned forward. In his hand was a leather folder, worn from age and stained with perspiration. His hands undid a leather thong, flipped the flap back, and seized a faded, yellow scrap of old newspaper.

"Here read it yourself."

I took the November 28, 1907, **Minneapolis Journal** page and read the following obituary:

Deadwood, S.D. — 'Buster' the best known dog in the Black Hills, is dead. He was the property of W. L. McLaughlin, the manager of the Mogul Mining Company. 'Buster's' pet trick was to watch the eastern mail sacks as they were thrown from incoming trains and permit no one but the mail clerk to touch them. He was the only passholder on the Burlington railroad who was not an employee and used to ride to and from the Mogul mill at Pluma at will, occupying one of the seats as a regular passenger."

My nameless friend began to get up. "I gotta get home," he said.

But I was too anxious to hear more. There were still Captain Crawford, Kitty Leroy, Belle Siddows, Baptiste Pourier, the prize fight between the "Belfast Chicken and Cook the Kid" that lasted 52 rounds, the vigilantes that hung Harry Tuttle the horsethief, Judges Bennett and Kuykendall, Black Hills Ben, and Deadwood Dick.

I reached out. "One more story please," I begged. "Tell me about Deadwood Dick."

"Well, once in our Deadwood rodeo a black cowboy named Nat Love did so well in every event that they named him Deadwood Dick."

"No, that's not the story. I want to know about the real Deadwood Dick."

I reached to my back pocket and brought out the crumpled paperback book. I opened **The Double Daggers; or Deadwood Dick's Defiance** and read:

A sudden shot rang out and the masked man uttered a cry of pain and dropped his pistol as he clutched at his injured wrist.

"Thought you had the drop on me, did you, you sneaking, cowardly villain?"

The handsome, athletic stagedriver bounded gracefully back into the seat of the stagecoach, brandishing the revolver that had appeared as if by magic in his hand. "Stand aside, all of you. The man you see before you is none other than Deadwood Dick himself!"

"You are Deadwood Dick, the fearless road agent?" cried the other masked bandits, who fell back before his bold gaze. "But how is it you are driving the stagecoach?"

"A errand of mercy!" cried Deadwood Dick. "This coach must be pulled into Deadwood by these faithful horses ere midnight! And any man who stands in my way shall die like a dog!" Thus saying, he cracked the whip over the horses' heads and sent them flying over the hill. Two of the masked bandits were foolhardy enough to pursue him, but Deadwood Dick's revolver spoke twice, and each bullet unerringly found its mark.

"No such guy," sneered the old timer.

"Wait," I said. "They say he visited President Coolidge and was at the World's Fair."

"That was an old stable hand named Dick Clark. He masqueraded as Deadwood Dick for the Days of 1876 and got so involved in the character that he even believed he was Deadwood. He posed for postcards, shook hands with famous people, and was a full-fledged tourist attraction. Actually, he was just a figment of Ned Buntline's imagination."

Abruptly, my companion got up, put on his hat, waved, and walked out of the No. 10 Saloon. Before I could ask his name, the bat wing doors swung in the haze. I looked up at the barkeep and asked if he knew my friend's name.

He set a shot glass down on the counter. "Deadwood Dick," he chuckled, and then moved away.

CHAPTER 17 # DEADWOOD TO CHEYENNE

As I drove southwest out of Deadwood on #85, I recalled the **Black Hills Pioneer** notice of June 26, 1877: "Mark Twain was at the Pioneer office yesterday." Fresh from the gold fields of the Rockies, this newspaper correspondent must have relished the excitement of Deadwood, but had he enjoyed his ride there? I was on the paved version of the Cheyenne to Deadwood Stagecoach Line. The forest here was dense pine. The scenery was magnificent.

Deadwood was a focal point for stages from Pierre, Bismarck, Medora, Yankton, Sidney, and Cheyenne. Individual routes changed with the whims of the mining fever. Each season would add new towns and drop deserted settlements. Many of the roads now crossing The Hills have been stagecoach or freight trails in their brief history.

Curley's Guide to the Black Hills, published in 1877, was the first official tour guide to the area. In it, Edwin Curley evaluated the routes:

It seemed to me that in going from Chicago to Bismark (sic), and thence to the Hills, I should be like a man trying to reach New York, by way of Hudson's Bay . . .

He listed the problems of travel as being difficult country, miry soil from snow melt, little good water, difficult ravines and too many Indians.

The Fort Pierre route was quite unavailable so early in the season, and therefore it was useless to canvass its demerits.

The Yankton direct route had many advocates, but the distance for overland travel was so much greater than by some other routes, without stage coaches for any portion of the journey and a part of the distance through such a forbidding region of bad lands, bad waters, and bad Indians, that I dismissed this route as unavailable.

Curley's route was the best choice by his evaluation, but read what he describes as the travel conditions between Elk Creek and Deadwood:

The greater portion of the way from Elk Creek to Deadwood was a very bad road, and while there were some weeds and bushes, there could scarcely be found a blade of grass. A large portion of the region traversed had been burned over eight years before, as I was informed by the telltale branches of the largest of the little pines, and almost all of it was dreary and dismal. There were, however, occasional gorges where fine cones of spruce, intermingling with the pines and patches of deciduous underbrush among the rocks, gave a very pretty effect. Our road was often both miry and filled with boulders.

My route continued through Cold Spring and on to Canyon Springs. The roads I took changed from blacktop to gravel, and even in the car I felt jostled and dusty. There must have been little comfort for the stage passenger. To absorb road shocks, which were almost non-stop, the rocker-bottomed body was hung on two thorough braces consisting of three inch thick strips of leather. These were less likely to break than steel springs, but caused the coach body to respond to each jolt or jostle with a nodding-forward motion like a violent pitch. Mark Twain called the Concord a "cradle on wheels," but the dry-land seasickness that it induced in others caused many passengers to get out and walk whenever possible. The jerk of the horses as they moved against their hitches heaved the body of the stage backward and then forward as if someone were giving it a push. People were crammed both inside and on top, and dust must have been a major part of the daily diet.

Canyon Springs Station was along Beaver Creek about 37 miles from Deadwood and 20 miles north of the Jenny Stockade. It was a relay station for coach horses. There were a combination stable and living quarters there. The valley is peaceful and unassuming as Black Hills valleys go, but it was here that the last and most spectacular stage robbery occurred. The stagecoach for this was the Monitor, an iron-lined rolling safe. The payload would be gold. At Beaver Station, Jesse Brown, Boone May, and Billy Sample, company shotguns, waited to go south with the coach. Gene Barnett was the driver, with six reins in one bare hand and a whip in the other. Gale Hill was on the boot with him, and inside were Scott Davis and Eugene Smith as guards, and one passenger, Hugh Campbell, a telegraph operator who was going to a new assignment at the Jenny Stockade.

Gene pulled the horses up in front of the log barn, but the stock tender was nowhere in sight. Gale called but got no answer. In the silence he slid down from the boot and began to block the rear wheels when he was met with a volley of gunshots. He was hit twice, but he managed to wound one of the robbers. A rifle bullet tore into him. As he lay on the ground, he wounded a second one. Smith was grazed and passed out. Scott Davis thought he was dead.

Barnett was used as a shield and Davis had to back down. Davis snuck away, went seven miles to get a horse, and then set out for Beaver Station. He got Brown, Sample, and May, and returned to the stage. Meanwhile, Smith and Barnett had been tied while the robbers used a sledge and chisel to break in. The robbers got away with $31,000. Dale Hill recovered. Hugh Campbell died and was buried in Mount Moriah.

Back on #85, I drove through the outer shells of the Black Hills into the rolling hills of Four Corners. There were red rock buttes and ponderosa ridges along the way and an occasional yellow rock cliff perched on red sandstone, like a marker for the route.

In Newcastle an old log building with tongue and groove construction sat amidst the official county buildings. Its role was to dispense tourist information. In the past it may have done the same for stage travelers, but its more important role had been as a stockade, hostelry, storehouse, blacksmith shop, dwelling and way station.

After leaving the broad valley at Newcastle I followed #85 south through sagebrush country. A few pronghorns added to the pleasures of the trip. Sage sparrows sang their intense mixture of song notes with an intermingled Bronx cheer.

Grooves in the grassland still mark the old stage route in this area. The land is a complex of small streams, including Lance, Old Woman, and Sage Creeks. The road dips into the broad muddy basin of the Cheyenne River. Here is Robber's Roost, the perfect place to waylay the coach, and on the far east horizon the Black Hills rise. The area near the crossing is deceptive. At first it looks as though no one could hide here on the grasslands, but in this country the rivers carve back-alleys and the flood plains are forests of cottonwood. Most important to the outlaw, the river sides are steep and the coach must be under control before plunging into the mud or the torrent of the Cheyenne.

D. Boone May was the agent in charge here when he wasn't riding shotgun. Frank James was one of the more famous stage robbers in this area, but he and Jesse got their reputations elsewhere. It was along these routes that Persimmon Bill led his notorious gang. Bill was a local character who seemed to have concentrated all his efforts in the Black Hills; and, consequently, he never reached the heights of western lore that he might have elsewhere. His only non-Black-Hills crime probably was the murder he committed, and was hung for, in his old home of Tennessee.

This route mixes many things; sagebrush and mountain, outlaw and marshal, pronghorn and longhorn on the parallel Texas trail, and even horned dinosaurs and bison, whose only link with the present is fossilized and bleached bones. Occasional mesas, their tops green with pines, offer the only break on the horizon. The grasslands seem to be a temperamental land that could exist at only one level. If the land pushed upward on a sandstone table, there were suspended pinelands; and if the layer below were exposed, there would be a valley cottonwood stand.

I turned on to a side road and drove past fenceline audiences of horned larks and lark buntings toward Hat Creek Station. An old building that had served as a wayside hotel still stands where the stage once stopped. Among farm buildings and ranch lands it seems almost lost. But then, Hat Creek Station was lost. The military had sent a group of soldiers from Fort Laramie to build a post on Hat Creek in Nebraska. They had gotten lost and built a station on Sage Creek in Wyoming, which was called Hat Creek Station.

This was the edge of the most dangerous outlaw and Indian territory, so the main building was equipped with a basement tunnel to the creek to get water during Indian raids. This was also one of the most complete stops for the passengers. Jack and Sallie Bowman ran a hotel here with telegraph, post office, brewery, bakery, butcher, and blacksmith.

At Lusk I wandered through the Stage Coach Museum and tried to imagine cramming nine people inside the Concord. It still seems impossible. The red and black coach must have looked like fire on the prairies as it moved amidst the smokelike clouds of dust from the horses' hooves. Driving the coach must have required a special talent too. The driver would hold three pairs of reins in his left hand, separating each pair with a finger to feel the difference in the horses' performance. Even in the winter the driver would go without gloves to "feel" the reins. With his right hand he would wield a stinging whip that would break above the horses with a loud snap.

The most famous of Luke Vorhees' reinsmen was George Lathrop, whose career began with stage driving in Kansas in 1861, bullwhacking in central California, and cattle driving. In 1879 he drove a trail herd to Rawhide Buttes for Luke and started to drive for him in 1881. He had the honor of holding the ribbons on the last stage on the Cheyenne-to-Deadwood route, and a monument is erected in his honor near Lusk.

This was the end of the Black Hills stage story and beyond was a story of other pioneers. Rawhide Buttes derives its name from a covered-wagon passenger who had been skinned alive. This was the Oregon Trail; its stories go east and west of the Black Hills. Across the Platte River was Fort Laramie, and beyond that was Cheyenne. At one time this area had been known as the Black Hills too, but now it is the Medicine Bow Mountain Range, and another story.

1880 train

"Wild Horse" Harry Hardin

PART IV —

ALWAYS THE HILLS

CHAPTER 18 # WANDERINGS

Dirt roads and wandering without a destination or map are fascinating ways to encounter the world. Places are always fresher and more exciting if you hadn't planned on finding them. In going through The Hills, I have collected many pleasures from just such a pursuit.

In Hot Springs the waters flow from the heart of the land. People seek health and veterans find a home. Hot Springs is apart from the rush, aside from the gold. Its streams steam in the stark white snow and form hoar frost fronds on leafless winter branches.

In a housing complex, a muddy mound sits isolated from the homes. Layer upon layer mark decades and centuries, and footprints of mammoths are suspended in millenniums. Tusks and teeth, hip bones and skulls are unearthed and the breezes of today blow in the eyesockets of yesterday to tell messages of survival to generations of the future.

Buffalo Gap is a notch on the horizon, a hole in the fence that keeps the riches of The Hills within. It is a dusty town of old buildings, banks, and mercantiles. The Gap has seen the mammoth change to bison, the bison to horses, the horses to cars, and now the town is an unpolished gem covered with the gentle wearing of time. Among the towns of The Hills, it is my favorite.

In Scenic, antlers glisten like cactus spines on an old whitewashed false front saloon and the sign says "no Indians allowed," but I can find no other non-Indians inside. A square stone jail stands isolated from the main street, its bars and hinges a pleasing rust-orange.

A park with covered picnic tables is surrounded by a crescent of rotting automobiles and bleached boards support a leaning sign that says "CAMPERS WELCOME." I look across a field from the park. A green church is outlined by the Badlands, and three stories of crosses rise like steps from the wooden door to the sky.

Old buildings surround a large main street. Custer's wide streets are overwhelming, I feel lost while crossing the main road. This is a place for covered wagons and bull teams. There should be wrestling in the streets, rearing horses, and mud to the calves. Cars seem out of place. This is the pioneer town of the interior, near Annie Tallent's home. Here is a town first named for Stonewall Jackson, then named for Custer as wars and heroes changed. Names like Fly Speck Billy and Mayor Bemis are part of its past, as well as its status as almost a ghost town during the heyday of the Deadwood gold fever.

Here is the gateway to Custer State Park and the wildlife of the Loop Drive, to Wind Cave and its subterranean maze, and to Jewel Cave and its spectacular crystal display. The town's wide roads are a gateway to many experiences. French Creek innocently flows over gravels that once glittered with gold, and granite domes rise behind the houses like the flexed muscles of a mountain god. Broad pasturelands and ranches dot the shadow of Harney Peak, and horsemen still ride with a majestic grandeur among the pine barrens.

Hill City is a valley city. Its personality is quiet and unhurried. In his classic guide to the Black Hills, Edwin Curley found Hill City a ghost town. He quoted Shakespeare's aphorism, "There is a destiny shapes our ends, rough hew them how we may," and noted that the founders of Hill City had "rough hewed to some purpose" one hundred and fifty neat and pleasing homes. He wished the people would return. Fortunately, they did return, and it is equally fortuitous that the city still retains some roughhewn qualities. Towns like Hill City need to retain their rusticness to belong in The Hills.

The pleasure of wandering is a freedom to react with your surroundings and to find pleasure and inspiration in ways that no one can direct for you.

CHAPTER 19 THE FOUR FACES OF PARADOX

No part of the Black Hills gives me more mixed emotions than Mount Rushmore. No single monument causes me to sort so many diverse thoughts.

As I drive the Norbeck Memorial Highway, the faces of the presidents loom at the end of every tunnel. They are perched at every corner. At first the tunnels and trees appear as impressive frameworks for a master artpiece, but with repetition the impact is lost.

I prefer to approach the monument from Custer where a blacktop lane sweeps between tall trees and rock buttresses. When the face of Washington peers down from its rocky heights, it seems more dramatic, more forceful.

Standing in the snow, alone amidst the trees, I look up into the four faces which rise with a godlike countenance above me. Mountain goats tread beneath the face of Roosevelt, the conservationist president, who was a rancher in the North Dakota Badlands before his career in a public office. He was a hunter and a cowboy, enjoying the rigors of life that this land could demand of a person.

It was in 1884 that T.R. came the closest to the Black Hills. In pursuit of a horse thief named Crazy Steve, he met Sheriff Seth Bullock in the prairies north of Belle Fourche. Roosevelt's autobiography describes the meeting:

We had had rather a rough trip and had lain out for a fortnight, so I suppose we looked somewhat unkempt. Seth received us with a rather distant courtesy at first, but unbent when he found out who we were, remarking 'You see, by your looks, I thought you were some kind of a tinhorn gambling outfit and I might have to keep an eye on you.'

This sparked a friendship between the two men that lasted their lifetime. T.R.'s sons spent summers with Seth, and the local cowboys took part in Teddy's inauguration.

Roosevelt's greatest impact on the area came not from his friendships, but from his conservation ethic. Roosevelt the hunter had watched the extinction of bighorn sheep in the Badlands, the slaughter caused by railroad market hunters, the slaughter of grazing animals because they competed with sheep and cattle, and the senseless slaughter techniques of transient sportsmen who butchered the herds of the west. He also witnessed gulleys where logging and grazing had stripped the land. These lessons were not forgotten.

He launched the Boone and Crockett Club, a hunter's group dedicated to big game animals and their preservation. He also established the first presidential administration to understand the need for preservation of wild lands and the need for a national forest system that would include tracts like the Black Hills. If the mountain goats should feel comfortable anywhere on this monument, then Teddy Roosevelt must be the place.

On a cold November evening I found the monument glowing in the spotlights. As I approached the deck outside the visitor center, my ears were assaulted with canned patriotic music. The darkness of the night was broken. Washington seemed to be gazing into the blackness beyond the lights and music. I was uncomfortable and disappointed. George Washington was out of place in this spectacle.

Washington had suffered the tragedies of Valley Forge, had known this country's pangs of birth, and had risen as its leader and hero. He was a king within a democratic republic, but he refused to be crowned. Here was a man who wouldn't accept a third term as president, who now sat in granite amidst a PR man's version of patriotism. I left because I felt uncomfortable in the sound and the glaring lights. I sought the darkness that Washington could only gaze upon.

This monument is more than a statue. It is a preserved piece of mountain scenery. Perhaps without the faces of the presidents we would not have the untouched forest and rocks that surround the figures and the buildings. If, in fact, the monument has preserved a part of the native flora, then Jefferson's head has a right to be held high. He was our agrarian president, a man who understood the needs for family farms and democracy, and a naturalist who studied both botany and paleontology.

Before becoming president, Jefferson wrote **Notes on the State of Virginia**, the first natural history survey of any state. He also engaged in the collection of fossils, and he made some outstanding geological discoveries. Jefferson watched the experiments of fellow botanist William Bartram and offered this fatalistic comment:

I long to be free for pursuits of this kind, instead of the detestable ones in which I am now laboring. Politics is my duty, but natural history is my passion.

My admiration for Jefferson comes from an event that combined his patriotism with his knowledge as a naturalist. In Europe at this time Comte de Buffon was the leading scientist, and his theories were regarded as law on much of the continent. He was Jefferson's counterpart, a naturalist with a provincial basis.

Buffon told his audiences in Europe that nature in the New World was inferior in all ways to that of the Old. Animals, plants, natives, and climate were all underdeveloped or degenerate forms of Old World life:

In thinly inhabited regions nature is always rude and sometimes deformed. The air and the earth overleaded with humid and noxious vapors are unable either to purify themselves or to profit by the influence of the sun, who darts in vain his most enlivening rays upon this frigid mass. All America can produce is reptiles and insects. The place can afford nourishment only for cold men and feeble animals.

The animals are tractable and timid, very few ferocious and none formidable. There is no North American animal comparable to the elephant: no giraffes, lions, or hippopotami. All animals are smaller in North America than Europe. Everything shrinks under a niggardly sky and unprolific land.

Imagine the indignation that Jefferson must have felt. Here was a man who recorded the bloom of the hyacinth, the fall of the puccoon flowers, the number of peas in a pint, statistics on cucumber production, the Aurora Borealis, and the number of blue teacups of jelly a quart of currant juice would make. This was a man who had a pet mockingbird on his shoulder while he worked in the White House.

In a letter to the President of Harvard, Jefferson penned:

What a field we have at our doors to signalize ourselves. The Botany of America is far from being exhausted, its mineralogy untouched, its natural history or zoology totally mistaken or misrepresented.

His **Notes on Virginia** was one answer to Buffon and the world. The cattle, sheep, and the Narragansett pacer (America's first new breed of horse) were also answers to Buffon. Jefferson's most effective reaction was more dramatic and less scientific. From France he ordered the complete skeleton of the largest moose the army could find. He then set this up in the office of the French ambassador.

Now the trails beneath the sculpture allow the visitor to view not only Jefferson, but the natural beauty he so loved. Nature is the least observed of the monument's assets, but it is also the most impressive.

Jefferson left us a legacy of the Louisiana Purchase that added this region to the United States. He also supported the Lewis and Clark mission which was not only an exercise in mapping but also a botanical trail of discovery. Jefferson explicitly directed the Corps of Discovery to acquire knowledge of "the soil and face of the country, its growth and vegetable productions, the animals, especially those not known in the U.S., the remains of any which may be extinct, the mineral productions . . ." He also wanted to know ". . . the dates at which plants put forth or lose their flower or leaf, times of appearance of particular birds, reptiles or insects."

In May and June the western spring beauty blooms in the forest beneath Mount Rushmore. It is one of the 200 species of plants Lewis and Clark identified. The Lewis woodpecker was named for one of the leaders, and the mountain goat was drawn in the party records. All of these are part of Jefferson's monument.

Abraham Lincoln's head stands alone, apart from the other presidents, and he too tells me a paradoxical tale. It was Lincoln the Emancipator who recognized the equality of races and the strengths of a union. It was also Lincoln who opened the west with the Homestead Act.

Now he tops the enigmatic symbol of a nation. His troubled eyes stare at Harney Peak, the symbol of the Indian world, and his head stands atop the most dramatic symbol of European dominance in the country.

CHAPTER 20 THE NATURALISTS

On Boland Ridge in Wind Cave Park I found a quiet solitude amidst the rush of August tourists. The sun was strong, and the sky deep blue with soft white billowy clouds. I left the clay road and moved among prairie plants that carpeted the ridge's flanks. A meadowlark's melody drifted across their wandlike tops, and I began to move up the steep sides.

The grass hills are deceptive about their height and grade. They seem mere bumps in the landscape's carpet until you begin to climb. Halfway up, I entered a grove of ponderosa pine and paused to let my breath reach the same altitude as my body. As I stood there, the trees began to talk, or rather they began to whine. From the clusters of needles on the branchtips came a long pulsating buzz. The trees seemed to be a chorus of invisible voice boxes, or cicadas to the entomologist.

The strange cicada has a masterful, but unusual adaptation for survival. Its eggs are placed in the ground, and the adult does not emerge for 13 or 17 years, depending on the species. That may seem like a long gestation period for an adult that will only survive a month, but there is a rationale for it. Animals that have peak cycles of production must not have their predators at their peak at the same time or the results could be devastating, so these cicadas outwait their predators. Most insect eaters don't live 13 or 17 years, and they have no way of leaving work for future generations.

The strange numbers 13 and 17 are perfect for another reason; they are not divisible by any other number but one, so animals that have three-, four-, or five-year population cycles will not peak with the cicada population except in rare years. For example, an animal with a five-year population cycle will match peaks with the 17-year cicada only once every 85 years.

As I went through the trees, the sound became so intense that my ears ached, but the bodies of these sounds remained hidden. I moved through quickly and in the process startled a pronghorn that stood up, apparently groggy, stared at me with that mulelike black and white face, and slowly ambled away. I reached the top of the ridge and startled two sleeping nighthawks. My presence sent them whirling into the air. Their pointed wings tipped back and forth in frantic indecision, their white wing-stripes flashed in the sunlight. In an instant both birds were gone. I thought of Thoreau's description of the nighthawk in **Walden:**

She looked so Saturnian, so one with the earth, so sphynx-like, a relic of the reign of Saturn which Jupiter did not destroy, a riddle that might well cause a man to go dash his head against a stone. It was not an actual living creature, far less a winged creature of the air, but a figure in stone or bronze, a fanciful production of art, like the gryphon or phoenix. In fact, with its breast toward me, and owing to its color or size, no bill perceptible, it looked like the end of a brand, such as are common in a clearing, its breast mottled, or alternately waved with dark brown and gray, its flat, grayish weather-beaten crown, its eyes nearly closed, purposely, lest these bright beads should betray it, with the stony cunning of the sphynx. A fanciful work in bronze to ornament a mantel. It was enough to fill one with awe. Another step and it fluttered down the hill, close to the ground, with a wabbling motion, as if touching the ground now with the tip of one wing, now with the other, so ten rods to the water, which it skimmed close over a few rods, and then rose and soared in the air above me. Wonderful creature, which sits motionless on its eggs, on the barest, most exposed hills, with its eyes shut and its wings folded; and after the two days' storm, when you think it has become a fit symbol of the rheumatism, it suddenly rises into the air, a bird, one of the most aerial, supple, and graceful of creatures, without stiffness in its wings or joints.

This land, with its rocky heights, its intricate caverns with boxwork and crystal displays, its full bloom on the prairie, and the secrets of the Badlands, makes me think of naturalists. Before me the land unfolds to the Cheyenne and White Rivers, and there the earth opens like a giant laboratory. Frank Lloyd Wright, the environmental architect who blended earth and structure, felt the Badlands offered him both a release from materiality and a confrontation with God. Wright was not the first to find inspiration in this "part of Hell with the fires burned out." Long before the gold seekers came to The Hills, naturalists came to the Badlands. Men like O. C. Marsh, Osborn, Hayden, Hatcher, and Leidy mystified the Indians with their requests to see "old bones."

I moved freely along the ridgetop, sometimes in trees, other times in sun-drenched meadows. Below me I could hear and see the long tailed magpies and a small herd of bison. In the distance was a coyote, moving stealthily, close to the ground. He seemed to be unhurried, yet covered ground quickly with his steady gait. The coyote is a symbol of the prairie and its abundance. It lives off the surplus and moves like the wind, steadily, incessantly.

I stood on a prominent shelf that jutted out to the east of the ridge and surveyed the surrounding land. It was rippled and dotted with plant life. I took in the grasses and pines, content to absorb the panorama, until I looked south, and south looked back. The animals were large. I thought perhaps a horse, at first, then I looked closer. Two elk were grazing in a stream bed. Their backs were turned to me. They had glanced back over their shoulders to see me coming.

I plummeted down the slope of my ledge and scrambled up the next convolution of the ridge's side. The last yards were on hands and knees, crawling to the apex where I could see the reddish brown "wapiti," the Indian word for elk. In the valley before me stood thirty-two elk, all ages, both male and female.

Had the naturalists Donaldson, Winchell, and Grinnell been impressed with sights like this when they accompanied Custer in his exploration? Did the elk, bison, and pronghorn leave a lasting impression on George Bird Grinnell, the zoologist? Did Grinnell remember things like this when he founded the first Audubon Society?

The "wapiti" moved down the valley. They sensed my presence; and as they moved from view, I stood and they picked up speed, first down the valley, then up and over another ridge. I moved along the side ridge to the main highland, startled a mule deer and a pronghorn, and found an elk antler.

I lifted the tined pole, and it was as tall as I am. The thought of neck muscles sufficient to carry a pair of six foot antlers is staggering. As I held it, I thought of its impressiveness as a trophy, but set it back down to be calcium for rodent's teeth. It seemed to belong here, and it would be out of place in my house.

The thought of trophies reminded me of Sir George Gore of Sligo, Ireland, who hired Jim Bridger for a guide, brought an arsenal of different guns, including 75 muzzle loading rifles, and a train of four six-mule wagons, twenty-one two-horse French carts, and two three-yoke ox wagons for a trophy hunt. His expedition lasted three years, cost $500,000 (1854 value, not current), included forty servants, some scientists, seventy saddle horses, three dairy cows, and approximately forty-five dogs.

He slept in a brass bed, on an ornate rug, under a green and white striped linen tent, drank vintage wines, and read English literature. His toll on the area

wildlife was 40 grizzly bears, 2500 buffalo, and uncounted elk, deer, and pronghorn.

This was not the last of the sport hunters in the bison slaughter. Eleven years later, William Drummond of Scotland, dressed in a white jacket and panama hat, left the prairie along the Platte River "strewn for miles" with buffalo carcasses. Buffalo Bill shot 4280 bison in 18 months, and the Grand Duke Alexis of Russia and his party shot 1500 in two days.

I looked at the bison below the ridge, a mere dozen where once I might have seen a thousand. They are unique to North America. They are fast, strong, and easy to see. The thought of walks in the grass country without bison staring at me across barrier-free space reminds me of my own fragility and recalls a sense of excitement from their presence.

The buffalo herds brought out the emotions of another naturalist who briefly glimpsed The Hills in the sunset years of his life. John James Audubon, bird painter, internationally acclaimed artist, set out for the west to work on his last major accomplishment, **The Quadrupeds of North America.** During his expedition through North and South Dakota, Audubon watched the bison slaughter. Sometimes they were killed for their tongues only; other times, for their meat and skin. On one occasion he was almost trampled by an infuriated bull when Audubon miscalculated his own age and speed. Amidst the excitement and his own specimen collecting, Audubon penned:

One can hardly conceive how it happens, notwithstanding these many deaths and the immense numbers that are murdered almost daily on these boundless wastes called prairies, besides the hosts that are drowned in the freshets, and the hundreds of young calves who die in early spring, so many are yet to be found. Daily we see so many that we hardly notice them more than the cattle in our pastures about our homes. But this cannot last; even now there is a perceptible difference in the size of the herds, and before many years the Buffalo, like the Great Auk, will have disappeared.

The remainder of his Dakota tour gave Audubon many pleasures and new insights, but the songs of the "meadowlark, red thrush" and other prairie birds were perhaps his greatest pleasures. As partners with Audubon were the two young bird artists, Isaac Sprague and Edward Harris. They and their contemporaries had big shoes to fill, for this was Audubon's last wilderness trip. He died just a few years later.

For other naturalists, this wildlife land was a collecting ground. Baird, Townsend, and Nuttall came close or hired trappers to furnish them with specimens, but they had no personal encounter with the land.

On a windswept saddle between two rocky points I found a prickly pear that looked like it was going to devour its own flower. The brilliant yellow bloom sat like a spot of sunshine between two barbed trap doors. The Dakota (Sioux) Indians called the plant "unchela" and played a cactus game with it. I pictured two young boys running through the grasses among the spiny cactus. A swift runner would take a plant and impale it on a ponderosa branch. The other boys would shoot their arrows at it; and when the target was struck, the holder would dash after the boy who had made the shot and try to swat him with the stick.

More important than the games were the foods that the fruit provided. The Indians would eat it raw, with the spines removed, or stew it. It was dried for winter food, and the peeled stems were used for dressings on wounds. Luther Standing Bear (Lakota) wrote:

The Lakota (Sioux) was a true naturalist — a lover of nature. He loved the earth and all the things of the earth, the attachment growing with age. The old people came literally to love the soil and they sat or reclined on the ground with a feeling of being close to a mothering power. It was good for the skin to touch the earth and the old people liked to remove their moccasins and walk, with bare feet, on this sacred earth. The soil was soothing, strengthening, cleansing, and healing.

Prairie turnip was eaten raw or boiled. Jerusalem artichoke roots were collected and eaten raw, roasted, or boiled. Wild licorice roots were used for toothaches, and wild cherries were gathered and eaten raw. The prairie was the Indian's cupboard and medicine chest.

Today we speak of natural cycles, the ecology of interrelationships in nature. Black Elk put it more succinctly:

You have noticed that everything an Indian does is in a circle, and that is because the power of the world always works in circles, and everything tries to be round.

The Sioux call themselves "Ikce wicasa," the natural humans. As a naturalist, it is a name I like; and if it were at all possible, it is a name I would adopt.

I bid adieu to a prickly pear bug, a well-concealed green insect that blends with the cactus color and even carries its own false thorn to hide it from the birds. Amidst the large things we often lose sight of the small and, therefore, fail to see the true world.

The day was passing, and I looked around once more before leaving. My eyes fell on the mosaic of green and brown lichens perched on the yellow rock. Once more, Thoreau came to mind:

During this walk, in looking toward the summit, I first observed that its steep, angular projections and the brows of the rocks were the parts chiefly covered with dark brown lichens . . . It was the steepest and most exposed parts of the high rocks alone on which they grew, where you would think it most difficult for them to cling. The temples of the mountain are covered with lichens, which color it for miles . . .

I wandered back toward the setting sun. My entire day had been spent upon one ridge, and yet I could not have seen or experienced more if I had hiked on ten such ridges. The richness of a day of solitude warmed me like it must have warmed the hearts of a thousand other naturalists. I had discovered beauty in one of its many homes in The Hills.

Mt. Rushmore

Begging burro

Mountain goat

Horsethief Lake

Homestake Gold Mine

Stalactite formations in one of the many caves

Steer wrestling at a rodeo

Black Hills farm

102

ALWAYS
H THE
ILLS

Deer

Elk antler

Petrified wood stump

Golden Eagle

ALWAYS
H THE
HILLS

Pronghorn buck

Bison

Canadian Geese in Sylvan Lake

Mule Deer

ALWAYS
H THE ILLS

Ponderosa Pines

ALWAYS
H THE
ILLS

Devils Tower

CHAPTER 21 # SONG OF THE LAND

In the early dawn hours, when the world seems coated in grey and the sky lacks definition, at the period when the morning light refuses to disclose whether the sky is cloudy or clear, I huddled in the April coolness on a dew-dampened grassy knoll.

The day birds were just awakening, the nighthawks' "peents" were dying down, and the whip-poor-will had ceased its chorus. A long winged silhouette moved silently across the grass tops and the short eared owl settled down. A chorus of coyotes sang quickly, and a chat tried a few notes from a bush. No songs were fluid yet, all actions seemed tentative.

Then a chickenlike bird strutted from a thicket onto the cropped dome. Another bird fluttered in, and soon there were a dozen. A pair of cowbirds squeaked, like a rusty hinge, in a tree above me, and a meadowlark gave the morning's first sweet song.

In front of me, the bird population had grown to two dozen sharp-tailed grouse. Individuals were staking out territory on the dance floor. A single male walked to the most prominent point, and lifted his wings until they made an arc from the ground on one side of his body to the other. Small purple air sacs emerged from his breast, the feathers behind his head stood erect, and his tail went stiff and upright.

The bird lowered his head, whined, and started moving his feet rapidly, pounding a dull throbbing rhythm on the ground. He moved forward like a jumbo jet that couldn't get off the ground with its cargo. A second male moved toward the first and began his dance. They met, leaped into the air, and thrashed the space in between them with their feet. The challenger gave room.

The hens clucked while the males placed themselves in squares with imaginary walls. A whining filled the air, followed by dancing males. The air was vibrating with tiny motors, and a poignant drama of success and sex was unleashed for the next hour.

When they came toward me, their orange eye tufts looked like morning fog lights. When they went away, their white-edged tails pointed skyward. Coos, clucks, cackles, and booms were the song of the morning.

All land has a song, a special essence that cannot be expressed in common speech. Some days the song is wind in the grasses, another day it is the wind winding through the needles of the pine. The drumming of a woodpecker, the echo of battling rams in snowy ravines, water tumbling over gravelly streambeds, and moments of pure silence in the black depths of a cave are all songs of the land.

The Indian described song as an extra power on earth. **If a man is to do something more than human he must have more than human power.** For this reason song was used for healing and for those other times that the Indian needed to call on a hidden reserve. Song was the breath of the spirit given form in man.

The Indian sang:

> The old men
> say
> the earth
> only
> endures.
> You spoke
> truly.
> You are right.

The songs the land heard sung back to it changed over the seasons. Songs were sung to cows, about cowboys, whores, and saloons. There were odes to the railroad, the miner, and the Oregon Trail. They even sang of the outlaw Sam Bass, and how his career was short.

SAM BASS

Sam Bass was born in Indiana, It was his native home,
And at the age of seventeen young Sam began to roam.
He first came out to Texas a cowboy for to be,
A kinderhearted fellow you seldom ever see.

Sam used to deal in race stock, he owned the Denton mare,
He matched her in scrub races and took her to the fair.
He fairly coined the money and spent it frank and free.
He always drank good whiskey wherever he might be.

Sam left where he was working one pretty morning in May,
A-heading for the Black Hills with his cattle and his pay.

Sold out in Custer City and then got on a spree,
A harder set of cowboys you seldom ever see.

A-riding back to Texas they robbed the U.P. train,
For safety split in couples and started out again.
Joe Collins and his partner were overtaken soon,
With all their hard-earned money they had to meet their
doom.

More appropriate to the times were the songs sung about the settlers and their lives.

DAKOTA LAND

We've reached the land of desert sweet, where nothing
grows for man to eat,
The wind it blows with feverish heat across the plains so
hard to beat.
We've reached the land of hills and stones where all is
strewn with buffalo bones.
O buffalo bones, bleached buffalo bones, I seem to hear
your sighs and moans.
We have no wheat, we have no oats, we have no corn to
feed our shoats;
Our chickens are so very poor they beg for crumbs
outside the door.
Our horses are of bronco race; starvation stares them in
the face,
We do not live, we only stay; we are too poor to get
away.
O Dakota land, sweet Dakota land, as on thy fiery soil I
stand,
I look across the plains and wonder why it never rains,
Till Gabriel blows his trumpet sound, and says the rain's
just gone around.

LITTLE OLD SOD SHANTY

I am looking rather seedy now while holding down my
claim,
And my victuals are not always served the best;
And the mice play shyly round me as I nestle down to
rest,
In my little old sod shanty in the West.
The hinges are of leather and the windows have no glass,
While the board roof lets the howling blizzards in,
And I hear the hungry coyote as he slinks up through the
grass
Round my little old sod shanty on my claim.

Captain Jack Crawford was known as the poet-scout. He was a resident of The Hills, who took Buffalo Bill's position when the old scout went to Wild West shows, and he was a friend of Wild Bill Hickok. Jack was the first Black Hiller to obtain fame for putting his words to verse. It is claimed that he put his contemporaries to tears (the reason why may be interpreted by the reader), but more importantly, he reflected the song and the style of the times.

FAREWELL, OLD CABIN HOME.

Ye folks of fashion and renown,
Who live in city and in town,
And who, 'mid luxury and ease,
Have everything the heart to please,
And every morning take your ride.

'Mid worldly pomp and fashion's pride,
At evening down the promenade
With lovely girls and hearts all glad,
And home — ah! that must be divine —
A little moss-grown hut is mine.

Where the streamlet's merry lay
Makes sweet music with its laughter,
Dancing, rippling day by day —
I shall hear it over after.

Where, from Harney's snow-clad crown,
Many rills come dancing down,
Where the speckled beauties glide
Swiftly through the silvery tide,
You may have your stall-fed steers —
I have lots of mountain deers.
You may have your hot-house greens,
I the good old standard beans —
Beans and pork. Sometimes he'd kill
A buffalo bull, would Buffalo Bill;
Then with chicken, grouse and quail,
And splendid soup from buffalo tail.

Oh, how happy, gay and free
O'er the mountains wild I roam —
Bank stocks never trouble me
In my little mountain home.

Up the mountain, down the glen —
Dangerous? Only now and then.
If a bear you want to court,
Take her where the hair is short;

His poem "Wild Bill's Grave" was sentimental and short. In a world of violence, mourning had to be short and strong, for there would be new demands the next day.

WILD BILL'S GRAVE.

On the side of the hill, between Whitewood and
Deadwood,
At the foot of the pine stump, there lies a lone grave,
Environed with rocks and with pine trees and redwood,
Where the wild roses bloom o'er the breast of the
brave.
A mantle of brushwood the green sward incloses,
The green boughs are waving far up overhead;
While under the sod and the flow'rets reposes
The brave and the dead.

In a hard land friendships were something special, whether with people or pets. Jack Crawford's St. Bernard saved him from dying in the quicksand of the Rio Grande. Jack never forgot.

HERO.
To my Friend H. K.

What'll I take fur that handsome dorg?
Wal, mister, how much are you worth?
A million! Ge whiz! That's a heap o' scads.
Wal, I ain't got a dollar on airth,
An' I reckon as how ye'll believe me, pard,
When I tell you I never struck ile;
But Hero's a great big bonanza to me,
An' he couldn't be bought fur yer pile.

Wal, no, he's never been trained, 'cause you see
    He's a kind of a self-made dog,
An' even when only a bit of a purp
    He wouldn't be seen with a hog.
An' he jest grow'd up with our blue-eyed May,
    An' they sported out thar on the lee,
An' one day I found that the noble ol' boy
    Had a load of affection fur me.

An' you'd like the story? Wal, 'tain't very long —
    Jest look at them big, honest eyes;
He knows as how I'm talkin' 'bout him,
    An' that's why he's lookin' so wise.

Sky Lines and Wood Smoke was the title of another collection of Black Hills songs. The poetry belonged to Badger Clark, an Iowan who came to the Badlands as a surveyor and worked in Lead as an editor. Clark lived alone in a cabin he built himself, The Badger Hole, and each year he welcomed tourists and school children to his home to listen to his verses. He would dress in whipcord breeches with a military blouse, and his goatee would pulstate beneath his broad-rimmed hat as he read his most famous works.

A COWBOY'S PRAYER
(Written for Mother)

Oh Lord, I've never lived where churches grow.
    I love creation better as it stood
That day You finished it so long ago
    And looked upon Your work and called it good.
I know that others find You in the light
    That's sifted down through tinted window panes,
And yet I seem to feel You near tonight
    In this dim, quiet starlight on the plains.

I thank You, Lord, that I am placed so well,
    That You have made my freedom so complete;
That I'm no slave of whistle, clock or bell,
    Nor weak-eyed prisoner of wall and street.
Just let me live my life as I've begun
    And give me work that's open to the sky;
Make me a pardner of the wind and sun,
    And I won't ask a life that's soft or high.
Let me be easy on the man that's down;
    Let me be square and generous with all.
I'm careless sometimes, Lord, when I'm in town,
    But never let 'em say I'm mean or small!
Make me as big and open as the plains,
    As honest as the hawse between my knees,
Clean as the wind that blows behind the rains,
    Free as the hawk that circles down the breeze!

Forgive me, Lord, if sometimes I forget.
    You know about the reasons that are hid.
You understand the things that gall and fret;
    You know me better than my mother did.
Just keep an eye on all that's done and said
    And right me, sometimes, when I turn aside,
And guide me on the long, dim trail ahead
    That stretches upward toward the Great Divide.

THE PLAINSMEN

Men of the older, gentler soil,

Loving the things that their fathers wrought —
Worn old fields of their fathers' toil,
    Scarred old hills where their fathers fought —
Loving their land for each ancient trace,
Like a mother dear for her wrinkled face,
    Such as they never can understand
    The way we have loved you, young, young land!

Born of a free, world-wandering race,
    Little we yearned o'er an oft-turned sod.
What did we care for the fathers' place,
    Having ours fresh from the hand of God?
Who feared the strangeness or wiles of you
When from the unreckoned miles of you,
    Thrilling the wind with a sweet command,
    Youth unto youth called, young, young land?

Of all the poets and authors who have struggled to listen to the land, perhaps the most lasting songs came from Walt Whitman's **Leaves of Grass.** Whitman visited Deadwood and walked the prairie sod. The visions of the Black Hills and the prairies had a strong influence. He felt the Deadwood sentiments in **From Far Dakota's Canons:**

From far Dakota's canons,
Lands of the wild ravine, the dusky Sioux, the lonesome
    stretch, the silence,
Haply to-day a mournful wail, haply a trumpet-note for
    heroes.

The battle bulletin,
The Indian ambuscade, the craft, the fatal environment,
In the midst of their little circle, with their slaughter's
    horses for breastworks,
The fall of Custer and all his officers and men.

Continues yet the old, old legend of our race,
The loftiest of life upheld by death,
The ancient banner perfectly maintain'd,
O lesson opportune, O how I welcome thee!

It was the prairie that gave Whitman his purest inspiration.

A PRAIRIE SUNSET

Shot gold, maroon and violet, dazzling silver, emerald,
    fawn,
The earth's whole amplitude and Nature's multiform
    power consign'd for once to colors;
The light, the general air possess'd by them — colors till
    now unknown,
No limit, confine — not the Western sky alone — the
    high meridian — North, South, all,
Pure luminous color fighting the silent shadows to the
    last.

I have looked at many songs and have listened to the wind down many a valley to try to learn the story of the land, but the story keeps changing, the song has many voices. While the rush of wind from a cave mouth may sing in my ear one day, my daughter's laughter floating over the bubbling waters of a rapid stream will be the song for another. This sprawling land has too many verses for one man to learn.

CHAPTER 22 # A CLOSING REFLECTION

I paused beside the road. Across the road from me, a sparkly schist reflected earthy stars of sunlight beneath a canopy of ponderosa pines. Next to me a road sign advised me of Rushmore and Custer and Hill City, and, in the direction I had just come from, Rapid City. Another sign, less informative, more gaudy, and literally shouting in the silence, proclaimed a site that should not be missed, a one-in-a-million spot complete with souvenirs.

This is the Black Hills, the center of the earth, a mirror of geologic history, a landscape painted dark by pines and surrounded by a rainbow of badlands. This is eagle country, a sacred land where the ancestors of the early travelers who had hiked across the Bering Straits could climb a peak and look for holy visions. It was here also that the white man could chase the yellow metal that seemed to be solidified sunbeams.

Cars raced past me, filled with people seeking the mystery of the Black Mountains. I sat down and wondered what they would find. The Hills are a siren, and all men share a weakness for her seductive call.

The Cheyenne, Kiowa, Mandan, Crow, Arikara, Pawnee, and Sioux all came here, and maybe other tribes as well. They came for the special qualities of the land and what it offered.

They were followed by Civil War generals, buffalo soldiers, gold seekers, claim jumpers, gamblers, gunslingers, Chinese, cowboys, sodbusters, sculptors, foresters, and tourists.

People came to climb, to walk, to cave, to snoop, to mine, to cut, to get away, and to attract others. Each pursued a different dream, but like the cyclone I first followed to the Black Hills, each dream was attached to the other, and they all took from the country.

The land remains a mosaic of peaks, valleys, ridges, gulches, prairie, and pinelands; but it is also a complex of roads, ghost towns, and tourist traps. Potential for oil surrounds The Hills; potential for uranium, gold, and other metals is within. The Indian stands outside the mountains, while the storehouse of his God is continually being removed.

The Black Hills are an island in the Great Plains. They are bountiful, but they are also limited. The problems that were here in 1876 are still here; they are just wearing a new outer shell. We must insure that the Black Hills are still available to future generations to seek visions. We must learn to be gentle on the land.

BIBLIOGRAPHY

Agenbroad, Larry. "Mammoth Site of Hot Springs South Dakota".

Audubon and Bachman. Audubon Game Animals. Hammond, Inc., Maplewood, New Jersey, 1968.

Bennett, Estelline. Old Deadwood Days. Scribner & Sons, New York, 1935.

Billard, Jules. "The World of the American Indian". NATIONAL GEOGRAPHIC. Washington, D.C., 1979.

"Black Hills, Once Hunting Grounds of the Red Men". NATIONAL GEOGRAPHIC. Washington, D.C., 1927.

Brady, Cyrus. Indian Fights and Fighters. University of Nebraska, Lincoln, Nebraska, 1971.

Browder, Sue. The American Biking Atlas and Touring Guide. Workman Publishing Co., New York, 1974.

Brown, Dee. "The Story of the Plains Indians". AMERICAN HISTORY ILLUSTRATED. August 1973.

Brown, Dee. Bury My Heart At Wounded Knee. Holt, Rinehart, Winston, New York, 1970.

Burnette, Robert. The Road to Wounded Knee. Bantam Books, New York, 1974.

Capps, Benjamin. The Great Chiefs. Time-Life Books, New York, 1975.

Capps, Benjamin. The Indians. Time-Life Books, New York, 1973.

Case, Leland. "Back to the Historic Black Hills". NATIONAL GEOGRAPHIC. Washington, D.C., October 1956.

Cather, Willa. O Pioneers. Houghton Mifflin Company, Boston, 1941.

Chancellor, John. Audubon. Viking Press, New York, 1978.

Clark, Badger. Skylines and Woodsmoke. The Chronicle Shop, Custer, South Dakota, 1935.

Clark, Badger. Sun and Saddle Leather. The Gorham Press, Boston, 1915.

Clowser, Don. Deadwood . . . The Historic City. Deadwood, South Dakota, 1978.

Colbert, Edwin. Wandering Lands and Animals. Dutton & Co., Inc., New York, 1973.

Crawford, Captain Jack. The Poet Scout. Funk and Wagnalls, New York, 1886.

Cummins and White. The American Frontier. Benziger, Inc., New York, 1972.

Curley, Edwin. Curley's Guide to the Black Hills. Chicago, 1877.

Custer, Elizabeth. Boots and Saddles. University of Oklahoma, Norman, 1961.

Dantee, Ross. Apache Land. Charles Scribner's Sons, Bantam Books, Inc., 1947.

Denig, Edwin. Five Indian Tribes of the Upper Missouri. University of Oklahoma, Norman, 1961.

"Devils Tower National Monument, A History". Devils Tower Natural History Association, 1973.

Dresden, Donald. The Marquis de More's. University of Oklahoma Press, Norman, 1970.

"Ecology, Then & Now; Black Hills". AMERICAN FORESTS, October 1972.

Faulk, Terry. Simple Methods of Mining Gold. The Filter Press, Palmer Lake, Colorado, 1969.

Fielder, Mildred. A Guide to Black Hills Ghost Mines. North Plains Press, Aberdeen, 1972.

Fielder, Mildred. Hiking Trails of the Black Hills. North Plains Press, Aberdeen, 1973.

Fielder, Mildred. Deadwood Dick. Bonanza Trails, Lead, 1974.

Fielder, Mildred. Poker Alice. Centennial Distributors, Deadwood, 1978.

Fielder, Mildred. Potato Creek Johnny. Bonanza Trails Publications, Lead, 1973.

Fielder, Mildred. The Chinese in the Black Hills. Bonanza Trails Publications, Lead, 1972.

Fielder, Mildred. Wild Bill Hickok. Bonanza Trails Publications, Lead, 1974.

Forbis, William. The Cowboys. Time-Life Books, New York, 1973.

Frison, Wilson & Wilson. "Hawken Site Bison Trap". AMERICAN ANTIQUITY, January 1976.

Garman, Mary. The Sundance Kid. Crook County Museum, Sundance, 1978.

Gilbert, Bil. The Trailblazers. Time-Life Books, New York, 1973.

Gilmore, Melvin. Uses of Plants by the Indians of the

Missouri River Region. University of Nebraska, Lincoln, 1977.

Guidebook and Roadlogs for Rocky Mountain Plains Field Conference. Friends of the Pleistocene, 1978.

Henry, Marguerite. Peter Lundy and the Medicine Hat Stallion. Rand McNally & Co., Chicago, 1972.

Herrick, Francis. Audubon the Naturalist. Dover Publications, New York, 1968.

Horn, Huston. The Pioneers. Time-Life Books, New York, 1974.

Hunt, N. Jane. South Dakota Historical Markers. Brevet Press, Sioux Falls, 1974.

Jackson, Donald. Custer's Gold. University of Nebraska Press, Lincoln, 1966.

Jennewein & Boorman. Dakota Panorama. Dakota Territory Centennial Commission, Freeman, S.D., 1973.

Josephy, Alvin Jr. The American Heritage Book of Indians. Bantam Books, New York, 1961.

Josephy, Alvin Jr. The Indian Heritage of America. Bantam Books, New York, 1968.

Lee, Bob. Gold, Gals, Guns, Guts. Deadwood-Lead Centennial, Inc., 1976.

Lisenbee, Alvis. "Laramide Structure of the Black Hills Uplift". Geological Society of America, Memoir #151.

McGillicuddy, Julia. McGillicuddy: Agent. Stanford Press, California, 1941.

McHugh, Tom. The Time of the Buffalo. Alfred A. Knopf, New York, 1972.

McLoughlin, Denis. Wild and Woolly. Doubleday & Co., Inc., Garden City, New York, 1975

McLuhan, T. C. Touch the Earth. Simon & Schuster, New York, 1971.

Milton, John. South Dakota. Norton & Co. Inc., Nashville, 1977.

Monaghan, Jay. The Book of the American West. Simon & Schuster, New York, 1963.

Morgan, Dale. Jedediah Smith and The Opening of the West. University of Nebraska, Lincoln, 1964.

Myers, J. Jay. Red Chiefs and White Challengers. Washington Square Press, New York, 1972.

Nauman, Dean. Vanishing Trails Expeditions. Wall, South Dakota, 1976.

Neihardt, John. Black Elk Speaks. Pocket Books, New York, 1959.

Nevin, David. The Expressmen. Time-Life Books, New York, 1974.

Nevin, David. The Soldiers. Time-Life Books, New York, 1973.

O'Harra, Cleophas. The White River Badlands. South Dakota School of Mines, Rapid City, S.D., 1920

Peattie, Roderick. The Black Hills. Vanguard Press, Inc., New York, 1952.

Petsch & McGregor. South Dakota's Rock History. Science Center University, Vermillion, South Dakota.

Pettingill & Whitney, Birds of the Black Hills. Cornell Laboratory of Ornithology, Ithaca, New York, 1965.

Progulske, Donald. Yellow Ore, Yellow Hair, Yellow Pine. Bulletin #616, July 1974, South Dakota State University, Brookings, South Dakota.

Rahn & Gries. Large Springs in the Black Hills, South Dakota and Wyoming. South Dakota School of Mines & Technology, Rapid City, South Dakota.

Robinson, Charles. "Geology of Devils Tower". U.S.G.S.

Robinson, Doane. History of South Dakota. Bowens & Co., 1904.

Rolvaag, O. E. Giants in the Earth. Harper & Row, New York, 1929.

Rosa, Joseph. They Called Him Wild Billy. University of Oklahoma Press, Norman, 1974.

Rothrock, E. P. Structures of the Black Hills. University of South Dakota, 1959.

Senn, Edward. Preacher Smith, Martyr of the Cross. Deadwood, South Dakota, 1939.

Simpich, Frederick. "South Dakota Keeps Its West Wild". NATIONAL GEOGRAPHIC. May 1947.

"South Dakota Historical Collections and Report". Vol. XXVII, 1954.

"South Dakota Place Names". University of South Dakota, Vermillion, 1941.

Spencer, Mrs. George E. Calamity Jane, A Story of the Black Hills. Cassell & Co., Limited. Broadway, N.Y. 1887.

Spring, Agnes. The Cheyenne and Black Hills Stage and Express Routes. The Arthur Clark Co., Glendale, California, 1949.

Sulentic, Joe. Deadwood Gulch, The Last Chinatown. Deadwood, S.D., 1975.

Tallent, Annie. The Black Hills or the Last Hunting Grounds of the Dakotahs. Brevet Press, Sioux Falls, 1974.

Thoreau, Henry David. Summer. Houghton Mifflin & Co., Cambridge, Mass., 1884.

Tolen, Ron. Black Hills Geological Guidebook. Northern Hills Printing, Spearfish, 1974.

Trachtman, Paul. The Gunfighters. Time-Life Books, New York, 1973.

Twain, Mark. Roughing It. New American Library, New York, 1962.

U.S. Government Printing Office. Mineral and Water Resources of South Dakota. Washington, D.C., 1975.

Vanderwerth, W. C. Indian Oratory. Ballantine Books, New York, 1971.

Vestal, Stanley. Jim Bridger. University of Nebraska, Lincoln, 1946.

Vitaliano, Dorothy. Legends of the Earth. Indiana University Press, Bloomington, 1973.

Wheeler, Keith. The Townsmen. Time-Life Books, New York, 1975.

Whitman, Walt. Leaves of Grass. New American Library, New York, 1958.

Wilder, Laura Ingalls. By The Shores Of Silver Lake. Harper & Row, New York, 1967.

Wilder, Laura Ingalls. Farmer Boy. Harper & Row, New York, 1968.

Wilder, Laura Ingalls. Little House in the Big Woods. Harper & Row, New York, 1968.

Wilder, Laura Ingalls. Little House on the Prairie. Harper & Row, New York, 1969.

Wilder, Laura Ingalls. Little Town on the Prairie. Harper & Row, New York, 1971.

Wilder, Laura Ingalls. On the Banks of Plum Creek. Harper & Row, New York, 1970.

Wilder, Laura Ingalls. The Long Winter. Harper & Row, New York, 1968.

Wilder, Laura Ingalls. These Happy Golden Years. Harper & Row, New York, 1971.

Mike Link is the founding director of Northwoods Audubon Center in Sandstone, Minnesota, and teaches for Northland College, University of Minnesota at Duluth, and Metro State University. He has worked as a naturalist since 1971 and as a writer since 1965. He is author of **Journeys to Door County,** **Grazing,** and **Nature's Classroom,** and has co-authored **Love of Loons** and **Boundary Waters Canoe Area Wilderness** with his wife Kate Crowley.

Mike's two grown children, Matt and Julie, share their father's love of exploring nature's wilderness and have backpacked in the Badlands and Black Hills. Mike now lives with Kate and her children, Jon and Alyssa. They share 20 acres in northern Minnesota affectionately named Dry Harbor Ranch for their interest in both sailing and the land.

Through his classes and his books, Mike seeks to express his profound sense of the human place in ecology and his love of the wilderness and American history.

Originally published in 1980, **Black Hills/Badlands: The** **Web of the West** was the second of six books that Craig Blacklock has photographed or cophotographed, including **Minnesota Wild,** jointly written and photographed with his father Les, and **Photographing** **Wildflowers: Techniques** **for the Advanced Amateur and Professional** on which he collaborated with his wife, Nadine.

Craig's other credits include the annual Blacklock calendars, **High West** and **Minnesota Seasons,** seventeen fine art posters, and inclusion in many books, calendars, and magazines.

Craig and Nadine provide nature photography workshops for several institutions each year. Their home is located in the woods near Moose Lake, Minnesota.